Nationalism and After

E.H. Carr

Nationalism and After

With a new Introduction from Michael Cox

palgrave
macmillan

ISBN 978-1-349-96037-8   ISBN 978-1-349-96038-5   (eBook)
https://doi.org/10.1057/978-1-349-96038-5

This Palgrave Macmillan imprint is published by the registered company Springer Nature Limited.
The registered company address is: The Campus, 4 Crinan Street, London, N1 9XW, United Kingdom.

Praise for new edition of *Nationalism and After*

"Nationalism supercharges the competitive, conflictual, and mistrustful dimensions of international relations. The idea of 'the nation' as the highest locus of loyalty and political legitimacy has for centuries constrained cooperation in the human interest. Resisting its divisive power is one of the challenges of our global times. The author of this book, E.H. Carr, was one of the most important thinkers about nations and nationalism in the early decades of the academic study of international relations; and by reissuing this book, Michael Cox and Palgrave have done the discipline a great service. In his substantial introduction Professor Cox begins by situating Carr's thinking in the context of the doctrine of 'self-determination' after 1918, particularly in the complex politics of Central and Eastern Europe. He concludes by asking us to think carefully about what we might learn from Carr's concerns about nationalism in the context of today's global challenges. 'A great deal' is the clear answer."

—Ken Booth FBA, *Distinguished Research Professor,*
Aberystwyth University, UK

"In this timely reissue of Carr's classic work on nationalism, Michael Cox brilliantly unravels Carr's complex views on one of the most contentious issues of the last two centuries. Demonstrating striking command of both primary and secondary materials, Cox demonstrates how a figure so critical of liberal projects for cosmopolitan governance could support an international order that superseded both nationalism and the nation-state. It is a fascinating story, and Cox tells it with great dexterity and élan. As the world's borders harden once again, this book makes for essential reading."

—Professor George Lawson, *Australian National University,*
Australia. Author of *Anatomies of Revolution*

"Like all his fellow realists, E.H. Carr paid much attention to nationalism and its primary manifestation: the nation-state. Grasping the relevance of *Nationalism and After* (1945), which lays out Carr's bold views on that powerful phenomenon, is greatly enhanced by Michael Cox's superb introductory essay."

—John J. Mearsheimer, *R. Wendell Harrison Distinguished Service*
Professor of Political Science, University of Chicago, USA. Author of
The Tragedy of Great Power Politics

"In his brilliantly written essay, Professor Cox does a masterful job of taking you from Carr's experiences as a Foreign Office official dealing directly with the challenges of nationalism in post-World War I Europe, all the way up through the interwar crisis, the war years and on to the Cold War, interweaving Carr's study of nationalism with his other abiding interests in IR and the USSR ... hugely informative and illuminating."
—Professor William Wohlforth, *Dartmouth College, USA*. Author of *America Abroad: The United States' Global Role in the 21st Century.*

"The welcome re-issue of Carr's penetrating study of nationalism is enhanced by Professor Cox's superb introduction, which is at once informative, insightful and fair—both to Carr and his critics."
—Philip Cunliffe, *University of Kent, UK*. Author of *The New Twenty Year's Crisis: A Critique of International Relations, 1999–2019*

"Probably best known today for his brief book *What is History?* E.H. Carr had an extraordinary career as a diplomat, academic, and semi-professional journalist, writing leaders for *The Times*. Though almost reclusive by nature, Carr was what the French call an 'homme des affaires'. He continues in death, to bitterly polarise opinion, mainly because of his views of the Soviet Union, rather than as one of the fathers of a realist approach to foreign policy. In his important introduction to a long-neglected volume, Professor Cox avoids these polemics, instead using cool and careful analysis of Carr's writings and the details of his service at the Foreign Office, to present a much more nuanced view of Carr, who truly deserves the epithet—rare in Britain—of public intellectual. Cox's introduction is a delight to read, in contrast to the leaden prose of Carr's massive history of the early Soviet Union, and he does much to shed light on what Carr had to say about nationalism and nation states in the international system."
—Professor Michael Burleigh, *Engelsberg Chair, London School of Economics, UK*. Author of *Small Wars: Far Away Places*

"Nationalism has returned as a critical factor in world politics. This timely re-issue of one of E.H. Carr's most provocative texts is a reminder of how his work speaks directly to us today. Professor Michael Cox's new introduction not only superbly captures the multi-faceted way in which Carr saw nationalism at work in the modern world, but it adds significantly to our knowledge of Carr's life and work. I strongly recommend this impressive piece of scholarship."
—Professor Randall Germain, *Carleton University, Canada*. Author of *E.H. Carr and IPE: An Essay in Retrieval*

"Professor Cox's superb introduction to E.H. Carr's under-discussed classic *Nationalism and After* is a classic in its own right which not only tells us much about Carr's wider contribution to thought, but is also an incisive and illuminating guide to Carr's ongoing engagement with the vicissitudes of nationalism and of the possible pathways to a world beyond it. In a time of resurgent nationalism in world politics, the reissue of Carr's slim but powerful volume published in 1945 is both timely and relevant."

—Aaron McKeill, *London School of Economics, UK.* Author, *Conceptualizing World Society*

"Written as the Second World War was ending, *Nationalism and After* is clear, pithy and pointed. Carr's analysis has worn surprisingly well and even his prognostications for the future bear a second look. In his introduction, Cox does an admirable job of setting the intellectual scene of the book, weaving together earlier and later work to give the reader a sense of the overall course of Carr's understanding of nationalism."

—Professor David Long, *The Norman Patterson School of International Affairs, Carleton University, Canada.* Author of *Towards a New Liberal Internationalism: The International Theory of J.A. Hobson*

"Professor Cox's very well written introduction perfectly places *Nationalism and After* in its correct and immediate context and within Carr's wider work and career as a whole … excellent."

—Sean Molloy, *University of Kent, UK.* Author of *The Hidden History of Realism: A Genealogy of Power Politics.*

"Michael Cox has done it again, with an in-depth reading of E.H. Carr that places the man and his work in historical context whilst bringing his insights right up to the present-day. Just as his introduction to *The Twenty Years Crisis* brought Carr's writings to a whole new generation of thinkers, this reissue of *Nationalism and After* will resonate with those attempting to understand the causes and consequences of the retreat to national borders and protectionism taking place across the globe. This is essential reading for a troubled world."

—Nicholas J Kitchen, *University of Surrey, UK.* Author of *Understanding American Power: Conceptual Clarity, Strategic Priorities and the Decline Debate*

"The introduction has all the hallmarks of Cox at his best, lots of vivacity, shrewd, knowledgeable, sympathetic but with a fair and discerning eye … and a good read."

—Emeritus Professor Alan Sharp, *University of Ulster, UK.* Author of *The Versailles Settlement: Peacemaking After the First World War* 1919–1923

CONTENTS

About the Authors

E.H. Carr joined the Foreign Office in 1916 and resigned 20 years later to become the fourth Woodrow Wilson Professor in the Department of International Politics at the University College of Wales Aberystwyth. There he wrote seven books including *The Twenty Years' Crisis* in 1939. The following year he joined the Ministry of Information before moving on to become the Assistant Editor of *The Times*. In 1945 he began work on his massive *History of Soviet Russia*. He was elected a fellow of Trinity College, Cambridge, in 1995. He is the author of the bestselling *What Is History?* (1961).

Michael Cox is Emeritus Professor of International Relations, London School of Economics, and founding director of LSE IDEAS. He is the author, editor and co-editor of over 20 books including works on the USSR, the end of the Cold War and of US role in the world system. His most recent books include a new edition of EH Carr's *The Twenty Years' Crisis* (2016); a third edition (with Doug Stokes) of his best-selling volume *US Foreign Policy* (2018); and a collection of his essays, *The Post-Cold War World* (2019). He has also recently brought out a new centennial edition of John Maynard Keynes' *The Economic Consequences of the Peace* (2019). He is now working on a new history of the LSE, entitled *The "School": LSE and the Shaping of the Modern World*.

INTRODUCTION

It is not too early to attempt an analysis of our contemporary revolution: It is a revolution against three predominant ideas of the nineteenth century: liberal democracy, national self-determination and laissez-faire economics. (E.H. Carr (1942), quoted in *Conditions of Peace*, London, Macmillan & Co. Ltd, 1942, p. 10)

E.H. Carr made his reputation as policy-maker, writer on international affairs and historian in an era that announced itself with a devastating conflict, continued with a revolution in Russia, went on to witness the near collapse of the western economic system in the 1930s, and concluded with yet two more wars—one decidedly hot and the other (at times) cold—which between them reshaped the world in ways that would have been thought inconceivable when Carr was born into the British Empire in the late nineteenth century.[1] To those who never experienced what Carr experienced, or who grew to intellectual maturity in more settled times, his answers to the questions posed by his age might now seem dated, problematic even. However, they did not seem entirely odd or idiosyncratic then. A classical Lloyd George liberal during and just after the First World War, an economic 'planner' by the late 1930s, a firm supporter of the alliance with the USSR during the war, and one of the more influential anti-

---

[1] For an earlier overview see my 'Will the real E.H. Carr please stand up?', *International Affairs*, Vol. 75, No. 3, July 1999, pp. 643–653. See also Michael Cox, *E.H. Carr: A Critical Appraisal*, Houndmills, Palgrave, Macmillan, 2000, and Michael Cox, 'Introduction', E.H. Carr, *The Twenty Years' Crisis, 1919–1939: An Introduction to the Study of International Relations*, Houndmills, Palgrave, 2001, pp. ix–lviii (reissued with a new Preface in 2016).

Cold War historians in the West thereafter, Carr lived through an epoch of revolutionary transformation which he reflected upon, wrote about, and sought in his own fashion to understand and shape.[2]

But if Carr lived through what were, by any measure, revolutionary times, he could hardly be described as a revolutionary himself. Indeed, his views on revolutions always remained decidedly ambiguous. Revolutions may have been critical transformative events.[3] However, they never changed society as much as revolutionaries hoped they would.[4] A classless society he once remarked was neither possible nor desirable;[5] and no society he believed could function without a ruling class.[6] As his closest friend, the Marxist Isaac Deutscher later observed, Carr may have admired revolutionaries from afar, but he did not really understand what motivated them.[7] A brilliant policy adviser when in the Foreign Office, later an influential member of Chatham House, a lead writer for *The Times* during the Second World War, and finally a Fellow of Trinity College Cambridge from the 1950s onwards, Carr may have come to be regarded as a dangerous heretic by some. Nevertheless, he always seemed to keep at least one

---

[2] See Edward Hallett Carr, *The New Society*, London, Macmillan & Co., 1951. In the US edition published at the height of the Cold War in 1957, the American publishers, no doubt in an effort to get Americans to read what was a left-wing book, described the short volume as a 'scholarly study' which described 'how western culture is proceeding in the direction of the robot civilization of Orwell's 1984'!

[3] See his *Studies in Revolution*, London, Macmillan & Co. Ltd, 1950.

[4] Carr paraphrasing de Tocqueville with approval wrote in 1956 that 'revolutions are less revolutionary than they appear at first blush, and interrupt the continuity of the nation's history less sharply and less radically than their sponsors like to pretend' This telling comment is taken from his chapter 'Russia and Europe as a Theme of Russian History' in Ricard Pares and A.J.P Taylor eds., *Essays presented to Sir Lewis Namier*, London, Macmillan, & Co Ltd, New York, St Martin's Press, 1956, p. 357.

[5] In 1933 Carr wrote that 'classless society' was the 'Achilles' heel of Marxism, and would, if ever achieved 'be as dull as the heaven of the orthodox Victorian'. See his 'Karl Marx, Fifty Years After' written under the pseudonym John Hallett, *The Fortnightly Review*, March 1933, p. 321.

[6] 'Carr wrote in August 1944 that 'No community can do without its "ruling class" or "leaders"' He went on to say that the 'public schools' in Britain had 'on the whole been particularly successful ... in training such a class'; and rather than being be abolished should be 'extended' by widening the 'the basis of recruitment' . See 'Memorandum From Mr. Carr to Mr. Barrington – Ward'. Carr Papers, University of Birmingham, p. 5.

[7] Isaac Deutscher, 'Mr E.H. Carr As Historian of Soviet Russia', *Soviet Studies*, April Vol. VI, No. 4, 1955, esp. p. 344.

foot inside the establishment without, it appears, ever becoming fully integrated into it.[8]

There was also something distinctly English about Carr. As he himself later confessed, he had a 'hidden preference for the English idiom' and a 'marked preference for the empirical over the theoretical'.[9] He did of course admire Marx and was much influenced by his view of history. Yet he never accepted some of Marx's key ideas.[10] Dissident he may well have been, but orthodox Marxist with a faith in the working class he most certainly was not. As Rosenberg has pointed, Carr always tended to look at the world from a state's eye point of view.[11] Even his leaving government in 1936 to take up the Woodrow Wilson Chair in International Politics in the University College of Wales in Aberystwyth was not to allow him space to agitate against capitalism, but rather to talk more openly about the conduct of British foreign policy. Needing more time to reflect on the world in a job which placed very few demands on his time, the decision to take up the post was however a decidedly odd one. Carr after all was no liberal, even though the Chair was funded by a distinguished Welsh family with impeccable Liberal credentials; and to add insult to injury, he was no great admirer of Woodrow Wilson either. Little wonder that the man who had played a central role in establishing the Chair in the first place—the formidable David Davies of Llandinam—was incensed and thereafter continued a low level campaign against the appointment![12]

Davies however was not the only person of note whom Carr managed to alienate over a long and argumentative career. In fact, he seemed to have what can only be described as a rare capacity for upsetting all manner of people including Winston Churchill when he was still Prime Minister

[8] Isaac Deutscher, ibid., p. 342.

[9] Quoted in Tamara Deutscher, 'E.H. Carr: A Personal Memoir', *New Left Review*, January-February 1983, no. 137, p. 84. Tamar Deutscher went on to characterize Carr, the great scourge of twentieth-century liberalism, as being in essence 'a nineteenth century liberal who had become exceedingly impatient with the anarchy of capitalism'! (p. 84).

[10] Shortly before his death Carr claimed that he had always been more interested in Marxism as a 'method' rather than the 'Marxist analysis of the decline of capitalism'. See his 'An Autobiography' (1980) in Michael Cox ed., E.H. Carr, *The Twenty Years' Crisis, 1919–1939: An Introduction to the Study of International Relations*, 2001, p. xviii.

[11] See Justin Rosenberg, *The Empire of Civil Society: A Critique of the Realist Theory of International Relations*, London, Verso, 1994, esp. pp. 10–15.

[12] On this particular episode see Brian Porter, 'E.H. Carr: The Aberystwyth Years, 1936–1947' in Michael Cox ed., *E.H. Carr: A Critical Reappraisal*, op. cit. pp. 36–67.

during the Second World War, the distinguished liberal historian of civilizations Arnold Toynbee,[13] the free market economist Friedrich Hayek who famously described Carr as one of the 'totalitarians' in our midst,[14] the best-selling novelist Rebecca West who seemingly detested him, and perhaps most interestingly of all, the democratic socialist George Orwell who later informed the British Foreign Office (in 1949) that while Carr certainly leaned towards the 'other side' in the Cold War, he was only 'an appeaser' not a communist agent of influence.[15]

The Cold War itself then pitched Carr into even more controversies as he fell foul of all those who did not share his views on Lenin—whom he came to admire, Five Year Plans—about which he was broadly speaking positive, and the USSR whose system he believed had to be understood not just denounced by what he liked to term western 'moralists'.[16] His enemies in this area were legion and included, amongst others, the influential Sovietologist Leonard Schapiro, the émigré political theorist Isaiah Berlin, the Polish-American expert on communism Zbigniew Brzezinski, and much later, the historian of Russia, Richard Pipes, an early adviser to President Reagan and another one of Carr's many formidable enemies on the conservative right. Even in death Carr managed to cause something close to hysteria amongst his opponents. One in particular, the British historian Norman Stone, just could not abide Carr,[17] and in one of 'the most violent diatribes' written by one academic against another accused the 'grim eminence' (as he called Carr) of all manner of sins.[18] Carr may

[13] Carr's many liberal critics are given a sympathetic hearing by Peter Wilson in his 'Carr and his Early Critics: Responses to The Twenty Years' Crisis, 1939–46', in Michael Cox, ed., *E.H. Carr: A Critical Appraisal*, op cit, pp. 165–197.

[14] According to one writer, 'Hayek' reserved 'special venom for Carr' in his famous polemic *The Road to Serfdom* published in 1944. Quoted in Andrew Gamble, *Hayek: The Iron Cage of Liberty,* New York, Routledge, 1996, esp. Chapter 4.

[15] Quote from Timothy Garton Ash, 'Orwell's List', *The New York Review of Books*, September 25, 2003.

[16] For a discussion of moralism in relation to Carr's work, see Raymond Geuss, 'Realism and the Relativity of Judgement', *International Relations*, 29 (1) March 2015, pp. 3–22.

[17] It has been suggested that one of the reasons Norman Stone was so vituperative towards Carr was because Carr had written a very tough review of Norman Stone's earlier book, *The Eastern Front 1914–1917*. New York, Scribners. 1976. See E.H Carr, 'The War No One Won', *The New York Review of Books*, April 29, 1976.

[18] Norman Stone, 'Grim Eminence' *London Review of Books*, Vol. 5, No. 1, January 1983, pp. 3–8. Stone continued his attack on Carr and other 'fellow travellers and devoted foes in the West' in a subsequent newspaper article. See his 'The evil empire: heroes and villains'. *The Sunday Times*, 1 September 1991.

have looked like a respectable member of a London club. However, he had annoyed too many people and had absorbed too much historical materialism ever to be fully acceptable in a Britain which after 1947 was engaged in a deadly ideological war against an enemy apparently animated by an alien Marxist faith.[19]

But even if Carr had a rare capacity for upsetting his enemies, liberals and conservatives alike, others of a more progressive persuasion tended to gravitate towards him in increasingly large numbers during the chill days of the Cold War. Certainly those on the political left seemed to be drawn to what this dissident yet established figure had to say about the world. Carr also managed to generate quite a following in the up-and-coming field of International Relations in the United States. Here his work on the deeper causes of the inter-war crisis became the starting point for much of their own thinking. However, even amongst some of his American admirers he did not find complete acceptance. Thus the father of the new discipline—Hans J Morgenthau—early accused him of having no moral compass,[20] while others attacked him for first having appeased Hitler in the 1930s and then Stalin in the 1940s and 1950s.[21] Meanwhile, back in Britain itself, those who did not share his world view continued to see Carr as someone who needed to be opposed rather than embraced, and at different points in time a galaxy of the great and the good accused him of committing all sorts of ideological crimes from being an 'amoral objectivist' to always siding with the 'winners' of history.[22] Even his biographer came under attack, not because he was uncritical of Carr, but rather because he was not critical enough. Jonathan Haslam's book on Carr was hardly an apologia.[23] However, even his attempt to be objective only seemed to provoke yet another outburst from an illustrious group of reviewers who said little about the book but a great deal about Carr, this 'very cold fish'[24] according

---

[19] Edward Acton, 'Historical Bees Abuzz', *The Sunday Times*, 13 February 1983.

[20] See Hans J. Morgenthau, 'The Political Science of E.H. Carr', *World Politics*, Volume 1, Issue 1, October 1948, pp. 127–134.

[21] See, for example, W.T. R Fox, 'E.H. Carr and political realism: Vision and revision', *Review of International Studies*, 1985, 11, 1, pp. 1–16.

[22] 'It is the author's unhesitating identification of history with the victorious cause' which marked Carr out as an historian, argued H.R. Trevor-Roper in his 'E.H. Carr's Success Story' *Encounter*, May 1962, pp. 69–76.

[23] See Jonathan Haslam, *The Vices of Integrity: E.H Carr: 1892–1982*, London Verso, 1999.

[24] Richard Pipes, 'A Very Cold Fish' *Times Literary Supplement*, 10 September. 1999.

to one writer and a 'cold blooded colossus'[25] according to another, who had devoted his life to defending the indefensible and sowing seeds of illusion in a collectivist future that had only brought misery and tragedy in its wake.[26]

Yet there was little to indicate that this most middle class of young men from a distinctly sheltered background—'as a boy I was once taken on a holiday trip to Boulogne' he later confessed—who joined the Foreign Office because he could think of little else to do with his considerable talents, would later be dubbed an 'active danger'[27] (during the Second World War) and one of 'the most dangerous'[28] scholars working in Britain after it. There was every indication however that he would one day become a serious author, even when marking time in the Foreign Office.[29] Indeed, his first three books and the bulk of the fourth—all published in the remarkably short space of six years—were written when he was still in its employ. Biographies each, they dealt, perhaps significantly, with four restless outsiders: the Russian novelist Dostoevksy,[30] the revolutionary exile Alexander Herzen,[31] Karl Marx[32] and the anarchist Michael Bakunin.[33]

Carr then turned his attention to international affairs, and between 1937 and 1946, while holding the Chair in Aberystwyth, wrote or helped author no less than seven volumes: one a popular study of the inter-war years (his only book translated into Welsh);[34] another, a somewhat formal examination of British foreign policy (introduced by no less a personage as

[25] Daniel Johnson, 'A Cold-Blooded Colossus' *Daily Telegraph*, 31 July 1999.

[26] For one of the less vituperative but still fairly critical reviews, of the Haslam biography, see Anatol Lieven, 'British Chill', *London Review of Books*, Vol. 22, No. 16, 24 August 2000. See also my reply in the same publication in the Letters section of Volume 22, No. 17, 7 September 2000.

[27] See Charles Jones, *E.H. Carr and International Relations: A Duty to Lie*, Cambridge, Cambridge University Press, 1998, pp. 97–120.

[28] The remark about Carr being dangerous was reported to have been made by Zbigniew Brzezinski. Quoted in Haslam, op.cit, p. 223.

[29] For a guide to Carr's own work see my 'A Brief Guide to the Writings of E.H. Carr' in Michael Cox ed., *The Twenty Years Crisis, 1919–1939*, (2016 edition), pp. lxxv–lxxix.

[30] E.H. Carr, *Dostoevesky, 1821–1881*. London, Unwin Books, 1931.

[31] E.H. Carr, *The Romantic Exiles: A Nineteenth Century Portrait Gallery*, London: Victor Gollancz, 1933.

[32] E.H. Carr, *Karl Marx: A Study in Fanaticism*, London: Dent, 1934.

[33] E.H. Carr, *Michael Bakunin*, London: Macmillan, 1937.

[34] E.H. Carr, *International Relations Since the Peace Treaties*, London: Macmillan, 1937.

the Foreign Secretary, Lord Halifax);[35] a third (a group study) on nationalism;[36] a fourth on how to build a more peaceful world;[37] a fifth (reprinted here) entitled *Nationalism and After*;[38] another on the impact the USSR had had on the West;[39] and of course his most famous study of all, *The Twenty Years' Crisis* published on the eve of the Second World War. Carr thereafter had very little of note to say on international politics as such.[40] He did of course go on to write fourteen volumes on the early history of the USSR, on which more later; and he did publish at least two popular studies—one entitled *The New Society* published in 1951, and the other *What Is History?*[41] which turned out to be his most successful book ever (possibly because it was one of his shortest!). But the emerging subject of IR interested him not at all. In fact, he later confessed to an Australian friend that IR was a 'rag bag' of a subject into which one could stick almost 'anything',[42] and to an American colleague, Stanley Hoffman, that he wished that he had had no part in getting the subject off the ground in the first place.[43]

Carr though was far more than just a controversial figure with a penchant for upsetting people. He was in a more profound sense a barometer of his times and representative of a generation of thinkers who felt that

[35] E.H. Carr, *Britain: A Study of Foreign Policy from the Versailles Treaty to the Outbreak of War*, London; New York: Longmans, Green & Co., 1939.

[36] *Nationalism*, A Report by a Study Group of Members of the Royal Institute of International Affairs, Oxford University Press, 1939. New Impression Frank Cass, 1963.

[37] E.H. Carr, *Conditions of Peace*, London, Macmillan, 1942.

[38] Interestingly, one of the other great works on nationalism written at about the same time as Carr's *Nationalism and After* in 1945 was Hans Kohn's much bulkier *The Idea of Nationalism: A Study in its Origins and background*, New York, Macmillan, 1944. It was reissued in 2008 by Transaction Publishers with a new introduction by the eminent American sociologist, Craig Calhoun.

[39] E.H. Carr, *The Soviet Impact on the Western World*, Macmillan, 1946.

[40] Though in the early 1950s he did write *German-Soviet Relations Between the Wars, 1919–1939*, London, Geoffrey Cumberlege, 1952.

[41] E.H. Carr, *What is History?* University of Cambridge Press, 1961. Carr's short volume was of course a very direct attack on orthodox history. In one letter he wrote that he had been 'looking for some time for an opportunity to deliver a broadside on history in general'. Letter to R.W. Davis, Carr Papers, Birmingham University, December 9, 1959.

[42] Quote from a letter to the Australian Sovietologist, Sheila Fitzpatrick, 4 November 1971. Carr added that 'Charles Manning's attempt to turn' IR 'into some sort of self-contained subject' (at LSE) 'was a fiasco'. Carr Papers, The University of Birmingham.

[43] The attempt to establish a 'science of international relations' had failed he admitted and that he himself was 'not particularly proud' of the part he had played in 'starting this business'. See Carr Papers, The University of Birmingham.

traditional liberal answers which might have made a great deal of sense in one century made little at all in another.[44] He was hardly alone in doing so. As one of the many thinkers who influenced Carr observed at the time, Europe was not just in disarray after the First World War, its very life was in danger.[45] Keynes may have been a radical liberal looking to save the liberal order from itself and Carr a collectivist who came to believe that it was beyond redemption.[46] Nevertheless, both agreed that the crisis which the world was facing in the inter-war years was a profound one. Some major reordering was therefore essential. This led Keynes to rethink economics and economic policy; Carr though believed it would require something much more fundamental: namely the creation of something like a new deal in Europe accompanied by a complete reconstruction of the state system. As he pointed out in *The Twenty Years' Crisis*, nothing was 'permanent in history' including 'the territorial unit of power' known as the nation-state. This unit had not been around for ever; in fact, power before the nation-state had been organized 'on grounds other than those of territorial sovereignty'. It would be 'rash' and profoundly ahistorical therefore to assume it would remain 'the ultimate group unit of human society' into the foreseeable future.[47]

Unsurprisingly, Carr's argument about the transitory and historically evolving character of the nation-state has generated quite a debate, even amongst more sympathetic scholars.[48] Certainly, his call for radical change in the international system was, and is, not one which has recommended

---

[44] Tamar Deutscher later characterized Carr, the great scourge of twentieth-century liberalism, as being in essence 'a nineteenth century liberal who had become exceedingly impatient with the anarchy of capitalism' op.cit, p. 84.

[45] See Michael Cox, 'Introduction' to the new centenary edition of John Maynard Keynes, *The Economic Consequences of the Peace*, Palgrave, Macmillan, 2019, pp. 1–48.

[46] See John Maynard Keynes 1925 essay 'Am I a Liberal?' in his *Essays in Persuasion*, London, Rupert Hart-Davis, 1952, pp. 323–338.

[47] The quotes here are taken from the 2016 edition of *The Twenty Years' Crisis*, esp. pp. 210, 211.

[48] The following works on Carr and nationalism still repay a close reading. Jan Jindy Petman, 'Nationalism and After' in Tim Dunne, Michael Cox and Ken Booth eds, *The Eighty Years' Crisis: International Relations, 1919–1999*. Cambridge University Press, 1998, pp. 149–164; Konstantinos Kostagiannis 'Mind the Gap between Nationalism and International Relations: Power and the nation-state in E.H. Carr's realism', *International Politics*, 50 (6), 2013, pp. 830–845; and Kaare Piirimae, 'Liberals and nationalism: E.H. Carr, Walter Lippmann and the Baltic States from 1918 to 1944', *Journal of Baltic Studies*, Volume 48, 2017, Issue No. 2, pp. 183–203.

itself to everybody, including, most obviously, a number of more conventional IR realists who appear to have taken from Carr that which they deem to be useful—most obviously his emphasis on the permanent struggle for power in a world of competitive nation-states—while ignoring almost entirely his argument that the world was for ever in flux and thus would not remain the same in perpetuity.[49] Nor did his persistent attacks on nationalism find much favour amongst those who were either sympathetic to nationalism or who have made their life's work the study of nationalism. Indeed, one of the more obvious reasons why his writings about nationalism and nation-states have over the years received far less attention than they probably deserve (a point made many years back by Ernest Gellner)[50] is that he appears to have had little time for the former while apparently declaring as redundant the unit upon which the international system had hitherto been organized.[51] As two of his friendlier interpreters have observed, Carr had, and has, many important things to say about international politics; but, at the end of the day, his understanding of the world led him to 'undervalue the obstinacy of the idea of nationalism' while underestimating 'the enduring power' of the institution of the nation-state.[52]

Whether or not this is an accurate or even a fair assessment is open to some doubt. In fact, a very strong case could be made—and I will be making it here—that Carr never underestimated nationalism (which might help explain why he wrote so much about it). Nor did he think it would be quite so easy to wave farewell to some kind of organized power in the international system. Moreover, even if he thought the number of states in

---

[49] For a good example of how one of the most influential and thought-provoking of realists 'reads' Carr see John Mearsheimer, 'E.H. Carr vs Idealism: The Battle Rages On', *International Relations*, 2005, Vol. 19(2): 139–152.

[50] Ernest Gellner 'Nationalism Reconsidered: E.H. Carr' *Review of International Studies*, Vol. 18, Issue 4, October 1992, pp. 285–293. This essay was based on the eighth annual E.H. Carr Memorial Lecture delivered at the University College of Wales, Aberystwyth, November 1991.

[51] For a fairly typical example of Carr's neglect in the field of "nationalist studies" see the well regarded volume by Umut Ozkirimli, *Contemporary Debates on Nationalism: A Critical Engagement*, Palgrave, 2005. For a sample of the journals on nationalism where Carr is also conspicuous by his absence, see *Studies in Ethnicity and Nationalism; Nationalism and Ethnic Politics;* and *Nations and Nationalism.*

[52] Quote from Daniel Kenealy and Konstantinos Kostagiannis, 'Realist Visions of European Union: E.H. Carr and Integration', *Millennium—Journal of International Studies*, 2012, 41(2), p. 224.

the system was set to decline, this did not mean that the system which followed would be any the less competitive.[53] Rather he believed that if a more rational, orderly world was to emerge after a world crisis which had nearly led to the death of what he defined as 'civilization', then two of the basic causes of that crisis—nationalism and the nation-state—would have to undergo a fundamental transformation. The real question then is not whether he underestimated the staying power of one or the resilience of the other, but why he came to believe that no international order worthy of the name could ever be constructed in a world composed of what he termed 'a multiplicity of nation states'?[54] After all, not all writers on international relations arrived at this radical conclusion; in fact, many of those he influenced most after the Second World War, especially in the United States, thought the thesis inherently implausible.[55] And they still do today.[56] Which raises the obvious question: why did this most empirical of analysts not given to wild speculation arrive at the apparently bold conclusion that the traditional state system was in dire need of reform?

As I will hope to show, the story of how Carr arrived at what some would still argue is a most dubious conclusion is in itself a fascinating one. Like most history in the twentieth century it begins with the First World War followed by the various attempts by the victors in 1919 to construct a peace. But it is more than just a story about a peace settlement which failed. Carr's analysis also raises big and important questions first about

[53] In a report to the publishers on Charles Manning's manuscript which was finally published as *The Nature of International Society* (Macmillan 1961) Carr wrote that while he found Manning whom he knew personally to be 'original and stimulating', he found the idea of an 'international society' to be an 'illusion'. The 'international game', as Carr termed it, has for the last 400 years been 'a creation of small and influential groups in the western world', though he added that there was 'no reason to suppose that it will survive the decline of these groups'. Macmillan Archives, 23 January 1961. Much later Carr wrote that 'No international society exists, but an open club without any substantive rules'. He continued that 'the study of international relations in the English speaking countries is simply a study of the best way to run the world from a positions of strength' Letter to Professor Stanley Hoffman, 30 September 1977, Carr papers, University of Birmingham.

[54] Preface to the Second edition of *The Twenty Years Crisis*, 15 November 1945, p. cxxii, 2016 edition. rs.

[55] See Stanley Hoffmann, 'Obstinate or Obsolete? The Fate of the Nation-State and the Case of Western Europe', *Daedalus*, Vol. 95, No. 3, Tradition and Change, Summer 1996, pp. 862–915.

[56] See John Mearsheimer's discussion of nationalism and realism as being 'kissing cousins'. http://www.sneps.net/t/images/Articles/11Mearsheimer_nationalism%20and%20realism.PDF.

the structure of the international system during the Cold War, secondly about the world after the Cold War when nationalism once again experienced a renewed lease of life—very much as it had done after the First World War—and finally about the increasingly divided world we happen to be living in today where the struggle would now seem to be between those, like Carr, who believe the nation-state is part of the problem and others who still continue to 'look at nation-states as something to be nurtured'.[57] It is easy enough to tell oneself that nationalism and the nation-state are simply facts of international life.[58] It is not so easy however to propose a way out of the problems caused by both. As Ken Booth pointed out many years ago,[59] Carr was at one very obvious level, a realist; however, he was a visionary too who through his work sought to reimagine the world, and one of the ways he tried to do this (as Andrew Linklater later showed) was by looking critically at nationalism and the nation-state, how the two together had damaged the possibility of establishing a true world order in the twentieth century, and whether or not it would be possible to establish a more equitable international community going forward.[60] Hopefully the republication of *Nationalism and After*[61] here will take us some way towards answering some of these big questions, and as a result encourage a much needed debate about a set of ideas and practices which continue to generate as many challenges to the international order in our own century as they did when Carr wrote about them in his.

[57] See Elizabeth Zerofsky, 'The Illiberal States: Victor Orban's vision for Europe', *The New Yorker*, January 14, 2019, p. 42.

[58] Steve Walt, 'You Can't Defeat Nationalism, So Stop Trying', *Foreign Policy*, June 4, 2019. https://foreignpolicy.com/2019/06/04/you-cant-defeat-nationalism-so-stop-trying/.

[59] Ken Booth, 'Security in Anarchy: Utopian Realism in Theory and Practice' *International Affairs*, Vol. 67, No. 3, July 1991, pp. 527–545.

[60] As Andrew Linklater has also pointed out, Carr's observations about the 'crisis of world politics in the first part of the twentieth century' are not just of historical interest but are relevant 'for contemporary debates which his reputation for Realism has served to distort'. Quoted in his 'The transformation of political community: E.H. Carr, critical theory and international relations', *Review of International Studies* (1997) 23, pp. 321–338.

[61] According to figures obtained from Macmillan, *Nationalism and After* (1945) sold 20,000 copies in its first print run and went on to sell another 10,000 copies over the next twenty years.

VERSAILLES, 'NEW STATES' AND MINORITIES

As independent nation-States they came prematurely into the world, and premature children are apt to experience a difficult infancy.[62]

One of Carr's closest collaborators, Bob Davies, once remarked that Carr was a man of many talents who achieved distinction not in one field but several.[63] However, as others have also gone on to point out, for someone who exercised so much influence in so many fields for so long, he never really had any formal academic training other than as a classicist. As he himself admitted much later, 'I did not really train as an historian, my training was in the Foreign Office'.[64] This in fact was crucial. As Richard Evans has pointed out, Carr's early intellectual formation was not as some detached academic teaching students and writing articles for learned journals, but as a 'Foreign Office mandarin'.[65] A close friend even referred to Carr as an 'intellectual expatriate' from the Foreign Office.[66] Furthermore, it was as a junior official after the First World War trying to find some kind of practical solution to what proved to be a most intractable problem, which initially brought him into contact with an issue that continued to preoccupy him for years thereafter.

Carr as we know entered the Foreign Office in 1916. However, within a year of having joined the FO he was having to deal with one of the great seismic shocks which came to define the history of the twentieth century: the Russian revolution. At this stage in his life he could hardly be described as a non-conformist with unconventional views. In fact, for someone who later wrote with a great deal of sympathy about the Bolsheviks, he displayed little of that when assigned the task of organizing the economic blockade of the new regime in Petrograd in 1917 and 1918. Experience in this field however led to him being assigned to a section of the Foreign Office dealing with 'north eastern Europe' which for Foreign Office purposes included the newly independent Baltic states (whose claims for

---

[62] *Nationalism,* op cit; p. 84.

[63] Bob Davies, 'Edward Hallet Carr: 1892–1982', *Proceedings of the British Academy,* 1984, p. 473.

[64] Quoted in a letter to 'Professor Hoffman', 30 September 1977. Carr Archives, Birmingham University.

[65] Richard Evans, 'Mullahs and Kulaks: He would bin them all', *The Times Higher,* November 9, 2001.

[66] See Isaac Deutscher, op cit., p. 342.

recognition Carr pressed), Poland (a country with which he developed a less than amicable relationship), Scandinavia as a whole, and of course, Russia itself. Having to develop policy towards this vast zone of instability where revolution was raging and bloody ethnic conflict had become the norm was no easy task. Nevertheless, by dint of hard work and attention to detail, Carr gradually became one of the few experts on a complex region about which many back in London knew very little and with the exception of Russia perhaps, possibly cared even less. Yet his Foreign Office reports were always meticulously researched and the conclusions arrived at invariably 'sensible and open-minded', very much like Carr himself.[67] His superiors were certainly impressed with the work of this young and up-and-coming member of the 'Office' who could pen incisive briefs and provide clear-headed advice on a whole range of topics ranging from 'The Question of Assistance to the Baltic States', the 'Political Situation in Estonia' and 'German Activity in Latvia' through to 'The Question of the Recognition' of the anti-Bolshevik government in Omsk (which he advised against), 'Events in Ukraine', and what to do about Soviet Russia more generally (don't intervene militarily he warned and don't assume that all the people in Russia were anti-Bolshevik).

But the issue which took up an increasing amount of Carr's time after he had arrived in Paris in early 1919 was that arising from his work developing a position on the 'New States' of Central and Eastern Europe. Appointed by the much more senior James Hedlam-Morley in early May to act as 'British Secretary of the New State's Committee',[68] Carr soon became a key figure, drafting many of the more important policy briefs and attending the numerous meetings that had to be convened as quickly as possible in order to come up with an agreed allied position. This was no easy job. Yet by early May an initial meeting had been convened with Carr in attendance.[69] This was then followed a couple of days later when a 'Preliminary Report of the Committee on New States' was presented for

---

[67] The comment about Carr was made by James Headlam-Morley who headed up the New States' Committee in Paris of which Carr became the British Secretary in May 1919. Quoted in Haslam, op. cit, fn. 55, p. 29.

[68] Sir James Headlam Morley, *A Memoir of the Peace Conference 1919*, edited by Agnes Headlam-Morley et al., London, Methuen & Co., p. 92.

[69] *Foreign Relations of the United States, The Paris Peace Conference, 1919, Vol III*, Washington, USGPO, 1943, p. 130.

'consideration' to the President of the United States.[70] The key question here was not whether the victorious allies would or would not recognize the new states; they had no alternative to do so given the facts on the ground. Rather it was how could the allies persuade or pressure the new states to treat their large minorities fairly? In this the allies had to walk a fine line. On the one hand, they did not wish to upset countries whose support they needed and whose role in containing communism was crucial. Nor in truth did they wish to see guarantees to minorities extended to all countries.[71] On the other hand, they still believed it was essential for the new nations to guarantee 'political and religious equality' for all those minorities who now found themselves living under the jurisdiction of states which had not existed before and whose new leaders they did not much trust or like.[72]

As anybody with even a passing knowledge of European history would have known at the time, the minorities 'problem' as it was invariably referred to was hardly a new one.[73] However, with the emergence of several new nations stretching from the Baltic to the Balkans after First World War, the issue had now become acute for the simple reason that each of the newly minted 'successor states' contained very large groups of people within their borders who owed no natural loyalty to the new states themselves.[74] The situation was potentially explosive everywhere; nowhere more so than in the new nation of Poland. Here ethnic Poles made up about just under 70% of the population, while its minorities (including

[70] Foreign Relations of the United States, *The Paris Peace Conference, 1919, Vol XI*, Washington, US GPO, 1945, p. 439.

[71] In a memorandum he had already discussed with Carr, Sir Esme Howard—later Ambassador to Spain and the USA—argued that protection for minorities is 'only required in the case of young and new States in Eastern Europe which have not a strong tradition of civilised government behind them'; this should and need not apply to what he called 'civilised' states' who could 'be trusted to deal with these matters by itself'. 18 April 1919. FO. 608.61. National Archives (Hereafter, NA).

[72] For one of the first attempts to analyse the problem see Lucy Mair, *The Protection of Minorities: The Working and Scope of the Minorities Treaties under the League of Nations*, London, Christophers, 1928.

[73] See Alan Sharp's excellent, 'Britain and the protection of minorities at the Paris Peace Conference, 1919' in A.C. Hepburn ed., *Minorities in History*, London, Edward Arnold, 1978, pp. 170–188.

[74] See Carole Fink, 'The Minorities Question at the Paris Peace Conference: The Polish Minority Treaty, June 28, 1919' in Manfred F. Boemeke et al., *The Treaty of Versailles: A Reassessment after 75 Years*, New York, Cambridge University Press, 1998, pp. 249–274.

substantial numbers of Ukrainians, Jews and Germans) constituted nearly 30%. But it was not just in Poland that there was a 'minority problem'. In the newly formed states of Czechoslovakia and Yugoslavia, Czechs and Serbs, respectively, constituted less than half the population. Meanwhile, in Romania the situation looked to be even more challenging; indeed, having already acquired a reputation for discriminating against its own Jewish minority since the late nineteenth century, the government in Bucharest now found itself in a position (of its own choosing to be sure) of having to rule over a very large number of minorities including a size-able group of Hungarians whose one and only desire was to rejoin the 'dismembered' Hungary from which they had recently been separated.[75]

In a perfect world perhaps none of this would have mattered much if the various ethnic and nationality groups in Central and Eastern Europe had had an amicable relationship with one another. But as Carr and his colleagues soon discovered, they clearly did not, and even as the war was drawing to an end, bloody conflicts were breaking out nearly everywhere with Poles and Hungarians pressing their claims against their various neighbours, Ukrainians defending what they saw as their rights against Poles, ethnic Germans opposing their incorporation into Poland and Czechoslovakia, and nearly all the different ethnic and national groups exhibiting their 'normal' hostility towards the oldest scapegoat of all: the Jews. Even the apparently more moderate Czechs according to one memo written at the time were behaving badly, and as result were 'hostilizing not only their former enemies the German Bohemians, also the Moravians and the Slovaks' but were behaving with extreme hostility towards their Jewish citizens as well.[76] It is perhaps too easy to talk about 'ancient hatreds' stretching back over the centuries. However, one thing was fast becoming clear as the war ended: that unless the great powers could impose some form of order on the region as a whole, then the explosive divisions within and between the various new states would not only make any stable settle-ment in Europe quite impossible in the short term; it also promised to be the source of new conflicts in the future.[77]

---

[75] See C.A. Macartney, *Hungary and Her Successors; The Treaty of Trianon and Its Consequences, 1919–1937*, London, Oxford University Press, 1937.

[76] The report was written on June 23, 1919 and can be found in E.L. Woodward and Rohan Butler, eds; *Documents on British Foreign Policy 1919–1939, First Series Volume VI, 1919*, London, HMSO, 1936, pp. 1–2.

[77] Derek Heater, *National Self-Determination: Woodrow Wilson and his Legacy*, Houndmills, Macmillan, 1994, p. 59.

It was into this 'ethnic and religious jumble' where 'one man's self-determination' meant 'another's disappointment' that Carr was thrust.[78] Very soon he became one of the go-to British experts on the subject. His advice often proved to be invaluable. It was Carr in fact who played a key role in March and April of 1919 in urging the allies to appoint an 'inter-allied committee' to 'consider the question' of all 'cultural minorities in E. Europe' and not (as the Americans seemed to be urging) the position of Jews alone.[79] On the more specific, thorny, issue of the Yiddish language he also helped clarify the British view, arguing successfully—against some opposition—that 'if the Jews in Poland want to talk Yiddish it should have the same protection as any other minority language'.[80] And much earlier it had been Carr no less who had drawn up an official paper outlining what would later become the formal British position on the minorities. He could not have been clearer: the new states really had no alternative but to protect their minorities. This he believed was not only the wisest course of action given that the various minorities were unlikely to move elsewhere;[81] it also made sense from a practical point of view. After all, if the minorities felt they were being treated fairly and well by their respective governments, there was at least a chance they would go on to become good and loyal citizens themselves. If not, there was an even greater risk they would become and act like disgruntled outsiders.[82] As Clemencau, the French Prime Minister, later put it in rebutting Romanian objections to having a minority rights Treaty thrust upon them—and they objected most strongly—it was not a 'question of encroaching upon the rights and sovereignty of any nation' but rather of guaranteeing stability and peace in Europe as a whole.[83]

---

[78] Quote from Sharp, op. cit., p. 177.

[79] Carr quote from FO. 608.61. 18th March 1919 (NA). See also Fink, fn 63, p. 265.

[80] Carr quote from FO.608.61. 14th March, 1919 (NA).

[81] Carr did not urge national governments or the allies to compel minorities to leave countries in which they now found themselves. What he did suggest was that 'in general it is desirable that States should hold out inducements to their nationals outside their borders to return to them'. However, 'any sort of compulsion is out of the question, and it does not appear that Allied Governments can take any action at all in the matter beyond a friendly hint of such a solution in the interests of future peace'. See E.H. Carr, 'Minority Nationalities', 20th November, 1918. FO 371/4383(NA).

[82] See Geoff Gilbert 'Religio-Nationalist Minorities and the Development of Minority Rights Law *Review of International Studies*', Vol. 25, No. 3, July, 1999, pp. 389–410.

[83] Jacob Robinson et al., *Were The Minorities Treaties a Failure?* Published by American Jewish Congress, Antin Press, 1943, p. 20.

Needless to say, the governments of the successor states were not easily persuaded, with the inevitable result that much of the time which Carr and his colleagues spent in Paris was in trying to persuade them that signing up to the various Minority Treaties was as much in their interests as it was in that of the minorities themselves. It was an uphill struggle. Not only were the leaders of the new states thin-skinned and easily moved to offence; having just escaped from under the tutelage of one set of great powers, they were in no mood to be dictated to by another, even if these great powers were the primary reason for them having gained their independence in the first place. As Lloyd George pointed out to the Polish leader Paderewski in one very heated exchange, the only reason Poland (like the other new states) now had their 'freedom' was not because they had brought it about themselves (in fact many Poles had fought on the other side during the war) but because there were 'a million and a half Frenchman dead, very nearly a million British, and half a million Italians' (he forgot 'how many Americans').[84] This however was not an argument likely to convince the leaders of the new states. No doubt they were grateful; that said, the sacrifice of the allies in the war against the Central Powers hardly justified imposing Minority Treaties on them. Not only did this imply a lack of trust; in their view it also represented a wholly unnecessary and uncalled for interference into their internal affairs.[85] Carr and others might try and argue that the best way to transform alienated minorities into contented citizens was by granting them special rights. They might also insist—as did the US President Wilson—that the peace of the world would one day be threatened if the minorities were not treated fairly. But this was not how the leaders of Central and Eastern Europe viewed things. To them this outside imposition not only constituted a form of great power bullying; more importantly, it represented a serious abrogation of that most basic of principles upon which the international system had rested since the seventeenth century: namely, 'the principles of state sovereignty'.[86]

[84] E.L. Woodward and Rohan Butler, eds; *Documents of British Foreign Policy, 1919–1939*, London, HMSO, 1949, p. 351.

[85] See Patrick Finney, 'An Evil for All Concerned': Great Britain and Minority Protection after 1919', *Journal of Contemporary History*, Volume 30, 1995, 533–551.

[86] Sharp, op.cit., p. 174.

Carr no doubt entered into these difficult discussions with what he would have regarded as an open mind; and being a liberal himself at the time he was more than happy to support the main claims of the new states. Yet the more he had to deal with their leaders, the less sympathy he found he had for them. As his biographer has observed, Carr may have been prepared to give the new states the benefit of the doubt when he first arrived in Paris. But as time passed he began to develop a 'dignified disdain' towards nearly all of them.[87] Poland, about which he wrote a great deal at the time, tested his tolerance to the limit. Here its leaders not only acted as if Poland could do no wrong, sometimes even blaming Polish Jews for being the cause of the many attacks against them. Its behaviour both at home and abroad was a cause of very deep concern. Poland may have been an indispensable bulwark protecting the rest of Europe from Bolshevism. However, this was no reason to turn a blind eye to what many on the allied side viewed as its provocative attitude towards its own German minority, its imperialist behaviour towards other nations, or the attacks then taking place in many parts of Poland against Polish Jews. Carr may not have harboured quite the same degree of animus towards the new Poland as his Foreign Office colleague, Lewis Namier.[88] Nonetheless, his less than benevolent view of the Poles were sufficiently well known back in London to render him somewhat suspect on the 'Polish question'. As one of his superiors later noted after having read a highly critical memorandum of his following a visit to Danzig, Upper Silesia and the disputed town of Teschen (the site of a short war between Czechoslovakia and Poland early in 1919) 'Mr Carr's well known dislike of everything Polish makes it necessary to receive his observations with the utmost caution'. Another senior person was perhaps more generous. Carr's report he thought was at one and the same time interesting and 'not without humour and insight' as well. Still, one should take note of Carr's 'anti-Polish bias' he concluded.[89]

---

[87] Haslam, op.cit., p. 29.

[88] Carr admired Namier and remained in touch with him during 1919–1920 when both were working for the British government. Born in Russian Poland, Namier was not only very well informed about Central and Eastern Europe but also deeply critical of what he saw as Polish territorial greed and their 'Jew baiting'. See Julia Namier, *Lewis Namier: A Biography*, London, Oxford University Press, 1971, pp. 136–152. On Namier's well-informed but sharply expressed views on Central and Eastern Europe, see D.W. Hayton, *Conservative revolutionary: the lives of Lewis Namier*, Manchester University Press, 2019, pp. 88–131.

[89] See E.H. Carr 'Notes on a Tour to Danzig, Warsaw and the Eastern plebiscite area'. June 1920. FO 371/3902 (NA).

Anti-Polish or not, even his most avid critic could hardly dispute Carr's facts, even if they did not much like the spin he put on them. Nor one suspects did most officials at the time disagree with Carr's more general observation that even if the establishment of the new states had been a necessity, it had not exactly laid the basis of order in Central and Eastern Europe. In fact, far from being some isolated critic standing alone, his belief that the difficult situation in Central and Eastern Europe had not been the result of a lack of sensitivity towards the new states but rather the attempt to construct stability by creating new territorial units containing large minorities became almost mainstream thinking after 1919.[90] As Alfred Zimmern (the first Wilson Chair) later observed, the attempt to build up a series of new states based on the principle of nationality might have seemed perfectly logical in theory. In practice however it simply did 'not fit the facts' on the ground.[91] Carr could not have agreed more. Moreover, as time went on, he began to discern a clear link between the ongoing situation in Central and Eastern Europe and the ideas of someone with whom he might have otherwise have had a natural political affinity: US President, Woodrow Wilson. Trying to build a new order on the debris left behind by the disintegration of the European empires would been hard enough. However, in Carr's view, it had been made nigh impossible because of the interventions of the US leader who was simply blinded to reality by an outmoded nineteenth-century way of thinking about the world around him.[92] Indeed, if one consequence of Carr's period in Paris was to leave him with a less than positive view of nationalists and nationalism—one which stayed with him for the rest of his life—another was to lead him to become highly critical of American diplomacy, less than convinced by its claims to be above power politics and increasingly sceptical of its ability to lead the world in a liberal direction when all the indictors suggested this could only end in tears.

---

[90] On May 17th 1929 the League of Nations published a 13-page report drawn up by James Headlam-Morley to examine the origin—if not the success or otherwise—of the various Minorities Treaties. See FO 371/1425 (NA). For the ongoing public debate about the Treaties, see the article published by J. Ramsay MacDonald 'Menace to Europe. Minority Populations: Should the Peace Treaties be Revised?', *Sunday Times*, 16 June, 1929.

[91] Quoted in Michael Cox, 'Nationalism, Nations and the Crisis of World Order, *International Relations*, Vol. 33, No. 2, June 2019, p. 254.

[92] *Conditions of The Peace*, op. cit p. 42.

WILSON AND SELF-DETERMINATION

When the President talks of 'self-determination' what unit has he in mind? Does he mean a race, a territorial area, or a community? Without a definite unit which is practical, application of this principle is dangerous to peace and stability.... The phrase is simply loaded with dynamite. It will raise hopes which can never be realized. It will, I fear, cost thousands of lives. In the end it is bound to be discredited, to be called the dream of an idealist who failed to realize the danger until too late to check those who attempt to put the principle in force. What a calamity that the phrase was ever uttered! What misery it will cause![93]

For someone who was later identified as being hostile to Woodrow Wilson, Carr himself arrived in Paris with no particular animus towards the American leader. Nonetheless, like many of his colleagues in the Foreign Office, he was concerned that Wilson, like the Americans more generally, had no clear idea of what they wanted or what they 'really stood for'.[94] Even before Wilson had arrived in Paris, officials in London were indicating a genuine concern both about his grasp of European geography not to mention the overall incoherence of many of his ideas. One member of the Foreign Office was even moved to comment that his various 'statements' about the world more generally and Europe more specifically were not only unclear but were 'capable of many different interpretations'.[95] Another, very senior figure in the Foreign Office, was more scathing still. Wilson's proposals about how to make peace were not merely 'nebulous' according to Sir Eyre Crowe;[96] they were 'dangerous make believe' which not only failed to take account of the balance of power but were likely in to add to Europe's many problems rather than solve them.[97] But it was the

---

[93] Robert Lansing, *The Peace Negotiations: a Personal Narrative* (Boston and New York: Houghton Mifflin Company, 1921, pp. 97–98. Lansing was Wilson's Secretary of State and is here citing his own notes from the Paris Peace Conference.

[94] See Carr's later comment concerning the 'basic ambiguity and uncertainty' of American policy coming into the discussions in Paris in 1919. Quoted in his edited volume, *From Napoleon to Stalin and other essays*. London, Macmillan Press, 1980, p. 143.

[95] See 'The Settlement'. November 1918. PID. FO 371. 4353.

[96] Sir Eyre Crowe was born and educated in Germany. Having entered the Foreign Office in 1885, he later warned in a famous Memorandum of a rising German threat and called for close relationship with France. In Paris he was one of the British plenipotentiaries where his fluency in both French and German proved invaluable. He later served as Permanent Under-Secretary at the Foreign Office from 1920 until his death in 1925.

[97] See 'League of Nations'. PID. FO. November 25th 1918 (NA).

idea of self-determination which seemed to raise most problems in the official British mind. They could hardly repudiate the idea given that Wilson himself seemed to lay so much store by it. On the other hand, like any 'general principle' it would be 'impossible' to make it 'the sole guide in dealing with every small portion of territory' in Central and Eastern Europe. As Headlam-Morley pointed out, 'general principles' are all well and good; however, in 'political affairs' they cannot be applied universally with the same consistency which obtains in mathematical and scientific work', and 'practical wisdom consists in recognizing this' fact.[98]

Whether or not Carr shared these reservations before the discussions began to unfold in Paris remains something of an unknown. Yet it is clear that the more he became embroiled in the affairs of Central and Eastern Europe, the more it became obvious to him that the idea of self-determination not only did not help much when it came to solving the minority question, but was encouraging the kind of aggressive nationalism he found himself facing when dealing with the leaders of countries like Poland, Romania and Czechoslovakia.[99] Nor he believed did the focus on territory and nationality do anything to address the very great economic challenges facing Europe at the time. As his contemporary Keynes later observed, 'the Wilsonian dogma which exalts and dignifies the division of race and nationality above the bonds of trade and culture' was not only leading Europe as a whole in the 'direction' of intensified 'nationalism'—something with which Carr wholly agreed—but would do little or nothing in furthering the continent's economic recovery. What made this all the more galling was that Wilson himself seemed to have no precise idea what the application of the principle might mean in practice,[100] appeared to adhere to different versions of the same principle,[101] and had no intention of applying the principle outside of Europe in countries populated by peoples lower down the evolutionary ladder (as he would have

---

[98] 'Note by Mr Headlam-Morley on the principle of self-determination'. nd. FO 371/4353 (NA).

[99] Carr later made the telling point that that 'national self-determination was a principle with awkward implications both for bourgeois democracy and for international accord'. See his *From Napoleon to Stalin and other Essays* op. cit.

[100] See Allan Lynch, 'Woodrow Wilson and the Principle of "National Self-Determination": A reconsideration', *Review of International Studies,* Vol. 28, 2, April 2022, pp. 419–436.

[101] Trygve Thronveit, 'The Fable of the Fourteen Points: Woodrow Wilson and National Self-Determination', *Diplomatic History*, Vol. 35, Issue 3, June 2011, pp. 445–481.

defined it) run by European states which he still regarded as being part of the wider (white) civilized world.[102] It was not just a case therefore of the British not really believing in self-determination as a 'right' (difficult to do so while running a vast Empire from London). Many Americans did not seem to have signed up to the idea either.[103]

Behind all this lay something else as well, of which Carr, like many others on the British side, were only too sensitive: namely, that the interests of the rising power across the Atlantic led by its apparently idealistic leader, and those of the British Empire led by men who were anything but, were not exactly the same. The United States may have helped finance the Allied war effort while helping turn the military tide in 1918. However, this did not make many on the British side feel any great warmth towards their so-called 'cousins' across the Atlantic. Anglo-Saxons together they may well have been.[104] However, this in itself was not enough to overcome the rivalry and distrust which existed between them. This in part had to do with economics. The United States might have become the indispensable nation in terms of loans lent to those actually fighting the war. But as the British sometimes liked to point out (and no-one on the British side pointed it out more than Keynes) it was actually making a great deal of money from the war. It then entered the conflict rather late in the day; then, once the Americans had joined the fray, they acted as if they were now in charge; and as if to add moral insult to economic injury—by the end of the war the United Kingdom was in massive debt to the Americans—they often talked of Germany and the Allies as being almost moral equivalents. Nor did Wilson help much in smoothing things over thereafter.[105] He may have been admired by English liberals and worshipped for a while by the peoples of Europe as a whole.[106] But there was still something about him

---

[102] For a wider discussion of the issue of race in world politics see Robert Vitalis, *White World Order: Black Power Politics. The Birth of American International Relations*, Cornell University Press, 2015.

[103] In 1950 Carr wrote to an American colleague pointing out that the British 'did not really believe in self-determination' and like the Americans 'had no 'notion of applying it to countries outside Europe'. Cited in Haslam, op. cit, p. 25.

[104] Duncan Bell, *Dreamworlds of Race: Empire and the Utopian Destiny of Anglo-America*, Princeton University, 2020.

[105] On British attitudes towards Wilson, see A. Lentin, *Lloyd George, Woodrow Wilson and the Guilt of Germany*, Leicester University Press, 1984, esp. pp. 8–12.

[106] See Laurence W. Martin, *Peace without Victory: Woodrow Wilson and British Liberals*, New Haven, Yale University Press, 1958.

which quite simply rubbed people up the wrong way! It was not just a matter of what he said either. It was the way in which he announced policy without any due consultation, including, most famously, his Fourteen Points of January 1918. His declaration of war aims may have sounded wonderful to American ears and helped him sell the war at home; nevertheless, it left both the United Kingdom and France 'perplexed and impatient'.[107] The British in particular were more than a little concerned as to what two of the points—the 'absolute freedom of navigation upon the seas' and 'free, open-minded, and absolutely impartial adjustment of all colonial claims'—might mean for British power. The French were equally confused. Wilson may have been a 'very great and good man' as Clemenceau once remarked following one very tense meeting in Paris. Still, this did not prevent the French leader making fun of what he, like Lloyd George, regarded as his extremely annoying tendency of laying down the law like some Presbyterian preacher. As Clemenceau caustically remarked about the former professor from Princeton, God had only needed ten points to shape the world: Wilson though required Fourteen!

British wariness about Wilson, and his about the British, did not fade even after he had arrived in Europe.[108] If anything, relations only got worse, in part because Wilson did nothing to flatter those who had borne the brunt of the fighting for over four years; he didn't even refer to the British (or the French) as 'allies' preferring the decidedly less intimate designation of 'associated powers'. Furthermore, in spite of all his fine liberal talk about not treating Germany as a pariah, that is precisely what in the end he did against considerable British advice. Nor was he prepared to do the one thing that might have made a liberal peace possible: namely write off the huge debts the Europeans had accumulated as a result of their heavy borrowing in the United States in order to pay for the war. Wilson may have sounded like an idealist. Nonetheless, this never stopped him practising good old fashioned power politics.[109] The Lord may have been on the side of the Americans and small nations as one wit remarked. This however did not prevent the Americans acting with ruthless self-regard when their own interests and money were at stake. Inside the lib-

---

[107] Quote from Lentin, op.cit, p. 10.

[108] For perhaps the fullest discussion on how Wilson was viewed in Britain, see G.R. Conyne, *Woodrow Wilson: British Perspectives, 1912–21*, Palgrave, Macmillan, 1992.

[109] A point also forcefully made by Adam Tooze in his *The Deluge: the Great War and the Remaking of Global Order* Penguin Books, 2014.

eral glove the steely hand of a great power in the making was not so well concealed.[110]

To a diplomat like Carr none of this would have come as much of a surprise. Carr was not naïve after all. As his later writings on international affairs clearly indicate, he was perfectly well aware of the fact that there was always bound to be a very large gap between what leaders of great powers claimed they were doing in the name of some higher principle and what their true interests really were. Nor as it turned out was Carr as hostile to Wilson as others appeared to be at the time. In fact, whereas Keynes left Paris a very angry man who later penned one of the more vitriolic attacks against Wilson—*The Economic Consequences of the Peace*—what Carr wrote later, though decidedly critical, was more inclined to see the problem in terms of a failure of ideas than the ignoble character of one very poorly equipped individual.[111] Wilson's 'tragedy', as he termed it, was not that he lacked imagination; it was rather that his views born in the age of Victorian liberalism 'no longer fitted the situation which confronted the world at the end of the devastating overthrow of the nineteenth century which we call the First World War'.[112] In other words, his beliefs were not so much flawed as outdated.[113] Even the Wilsonian 'principle' of self-determination was not entirely without merit. The problem with it, as Carr subsequently pointed out, was not that the idea in of itself was wrong; rather it was bound to prove a disaster in practice when applied to a complex region like Central and Eastern Europe in 1919.[114]

Carr did not even think that Wilsons's great institutional legacy—the League of Nations—was without value either.[115] The organization however

---

[110] In 1946 Carr made the interesting observation that whereas diplomats in an earlier age had rarely tried to hide behind ideals, Wilson had, with the result that there was a much 'larger measure of window-dressing or sheer hypocrisy' in 1919 'than had been customary in the franker days of nineteenth century diplomacy'. See his *The Soviet Impact on the Western World*, op.cit, p. 80.

[111] A good point made in Derek Heater, op. cit., p. 109.

[112] E.H. Carr, 'Change and Illusions' *Times Literary Supplement*, October 30, 1953.

[113] See Carr's review of a work on Wilson in *International Affairs*, July 1938, pp. 594–595.

[114] Carr, *Conditions of The Peace*, pp. 38–47.

[115] Carr wrote a brilliant piece on the League not long after he took up the Chair at Aberystwyth. See his 'The Future of the League', *The Fortnightly*, October 1936, pp. 385–396. Here he argued that the basic problem was not the idea of an international organization as such, but rather that the League of Nations as constituted was 'a League of Sovereign States' built on what Carr obviously viewed as the highly problematic 'basis of sovereignty' (ibid., pp. 388–389).

could only work in periods of quiescence and calm, and would only work if the great powers who actually ran the League were prepared to do something when aggression raised its ugly head. But they were not. As he himself noted, the League, for which he retained some affection, actually did some good things.[116] The problem was not so much the organization for which Wilson had originally argued, but rather what Carr termed those 'metaphysicians in Geneva' who continued to cling to the belief that fine words, well-crafted declarations and vague threats to impose economic sanctions would deter aggression.[117] As he later pointed out in his Inaugural Lecture delivered in Aberystwyth after he had taken up the Chair there in 1936, the League might have been 'one of the most striking and encouraging facts in the world of international politics since the War'. Sadly however it was based on a faith in collective security and a peace settlement which could no longer be defended by the 1930s. A new way of dealing with the world and its problems would have to be found, not one which took as its starting-point Versailles and the 'putrefying corpse of 1919'.[118]

NATIONALISM THE WORLD'S BANE

The solution of the Internationalists may be a bad one; it is at least a solution which moves forward with the clock. The solution of the ultra-Nationalists is merely to put the clock back.[119]

As we have seen, the starting point for Carr's critique of nationalism was what he himself experienced as a young diplomat in Paris. Engaging with leaders from the new states and attempting to reconcile their demands with those of the many minorities dotted all over Central and Eastern Europe was, as he found out, an almost impossible task which only

[116] See his anonymized article 'The League of Nations' *The Times Literary Supplement*, April 11 1952, where he contrasts the League favourably with the United Nations.

[117] In one of his many book reviews written for the Chatham House journal *International Affairs* in the 1930s, Carr attacked all those—including Arnold Toynbee, the author of the Annual Survey of International Affairs published by Chatham House—for assuming that economic sanctions without being backed up by military sanctions could deter aggression. See his review in *International Affairs*, March 1937, pp. 282–283.

[118] See E.H. Carr, 'Public Opinion As a Safeguard Of Peace', *International Affairs*, November–December 1936, Vol. XV, No. 6, pp. 1–17.

[119] Carr quote from 'Nationalism The World's Bane' *The Fortnightly Review*, Vol. 133, June 1933, p. 702.

managed to leave the new states resentful and the minorities discontented. Yet from all accounts, Carr himself had very much 'enjoyed the experience of Paris',[120] and apparently left the French capital with his 'Liberal principles still intact' and his reputation enhanced. Now based in the Latvian capital of Riga his attention now turned to Russia, from which vantage point he was able to keep a watchful, and no doubt critical eye, on Central and Eastern Europe where the situation remained anything but stable and secure. Battered by years of internecine conflict, and facing the uphill task of rebuilding largely agricultural economies, the chances of the new nations—with perhaps the one exception of Czechoslovakia—creating anything like the conditions for economic 'take-off' were very near close to zero. Given his own experiences in Paris, Carr was certainly not optimistic about the prospects. Protectionism and aggressive state intervention as practised right across the countries of the region may have boosted some economies there.[121] But self-sufficiency was no answer to the problems facing the region as a whole, which just about managed to get by through the 1920s only to be blown completely off course as a result the depression.[122] Indeed, by 1929 Central and Eastern Europe was facing a major economic crisis, and by 1930 near economic collapse as markets and credits dried up, leaving the 'whole fragmented region in an ever more vulnerable position waiting', (in Carr's own prophetic (and chilling) words), 'till one of the great powers has recovered sufficient strength to put the Central European house in order'.[123]

But if the coming of the great depression cast a very large shadow over the future of an already troubled region, it also raised in Carr's mind, as it did in many others at the time, fundamental questions both about the future of capitalism as a system and the nation-state as the foundation of international relations. Hitherto his interest in nationalism had largely been concentrated on one very disturbed part of the European continent; now, with the onset of the depression and the headlong rush by the early 1930s into national economic protectionism, the question in his mind was not whether small backward nations with few democratic traditions could survive and prosper by themselves—in his view they could not—but

---

[120] Haslam, op.cit, p. 34.

[121] See Ivan T. Berend, 'The Failure of Economic Nationalism: Central and Eastern Europe Before World War II', *Revue Economique*, Vol. 51, No. 2, Mar 2000, pp. 315–322.

[122] Hans Raupach, 'The Impact of the Great Depression on Eastern Europe', *Journal of Contemporary History*, Vol. 4, No. 4, The Great Depression (Oct., 1969), pp. 75–86.

[123] Haslam, ibid., pp. 33–34.

whether there could be any global order at all so long as the nation-state whatever its size, material capabilities or history remained in being? He began to provide something close to an answer in what Charles Jones has rightly called an 'eloquently expressed' piece published in 1933 under the *nom de plume*, John Hallett.[124]

The article, aptly titled 'Nationalism: The World's Bane', begins with what was later to become a standard Carr refrain, one repeated in much greater detail in later works: that nationalism in of itself was neither good nor bad, but was, instead, a historically constituted phenomenon whose impact on the world could only be assessed by looking at its role through time. The idea of the nation and a sense of national feeling could he argued be traced back centuries. However, in its modern form, it was the child of the Enlightenment which had then been promoted on the end of bayonets by that most universal of events—the French revolution.[125] In its mature nineteenth century form, it had then played a broadly progressive role allying itself to liberalism in its struggle against autocracy and reaction. But what he called these 'Siamese Twins' underwent a 'violent and decisive separation' in the lead up to 1914, most obviously in Germany and Russia where nationalism assumed an increasingly reactionary character. Woodrow Wilson for a while made it seem as if the nationalism and democracy could yet again be united; the alliance of an earlier age for a while seemed a distinct possibility. This was not to be however and nationalism—once more—proved to be a 'false idol' with 'feet of clay' which floundered in 'unhealthy' and less pleasant places, very much like those of Central and Eastern Europe in which Carr had been compelled to operate as a policy-maker in the years immediately following the war. Nor did things improve much thereafter with Italy descending into Fascism (a political movement that wore 'an ostentatiously nationalistic complexion'), Germany into National Socialism, and most of the states of Central Europe into dictatorship. In effect, nationalism and democracy had now 'become mortal enemies', and nothing the beleaguered League of Nations could do would be able put the two back together again.

---

[124] Charles Jones, op cit., p. 27.

[125] Carr much later noted that 'Nationalism, as historians and political theorists never tire of telling us, came into the world with the French Revolution and has remained a potent force for good and evil ever since' See his 'What Is A Nation?' *The Times Literary Supplement*, July 21, 1961.

It was not just nationalism however that was by now proving to be an impediment to progress; so too, according to Carr, was the nation-state itself. Indeed, not only was this particular unit of the international system a cause of increasing conflict; it was also becoming clear to all but the more obtuse that there was a growing contradiction between the nation-state and what Carr termed 'the economic exigencies of modern civilization'. To this extent, Marx had been proven right when in 1848 he had explained in crystal clear terms—ironically in a Manifesto making the case for communism—why the world market economy was fast outgrowing the nation-state. Marx might have been wrong to assume that class solidarity across frontiers would one day trump the bonds of nationhood. However, he was absolutely right to argue against the view (much loved by liberals) that capitalism and the nation-state would always be easy bedfellows. They were not. In fact, by the 1930s it was fast becoming clear that the whole international order was beginning to break down as nation-state after nation-state retreated into a dangerous form of protectionism which in his mind could only have one tragic outcome. Carr presented the problem in the shape of a question: could the world any longer maintain 'its plethora of national states large and small', all 'striving for national economic self-sufficiency' without this in the end 'leading us headlong' into another war 'more fatal, more far-reaching' and more 'destructive of civilization than the last'? The answer was obvious: the solution even clearer. A new order purged of nationalism and based on something altogether more rational than the nation-state, would have to be constructed.[126]

Carr though still seemed reluctant to draw the conclusion that a new international order was by now the only answer to the crisis facing humanity. Nor was it entirely clear what he thought the cause of that crisis was. Was it the behaviour of revisionist Germany under Hitler—or was it aggressive nationalism more generally? His answer, in the end, was a mixture of both. To address the problem posed by the first it was thus essential to create real incentives for peace: in effect appease Germany by agreeing to what Carr obviously saw as its legitimate territorial demands in Europe. Dealing with the second however would be far more difficult and would require a more fundamental restructuring of the international system. The two however were connected for both were symptomatic of a profound crisis within the wider liberal order.[127]

---

[126] See John Hallett, 'Nationalism: the World's Bane', *Fortnightly Review*, Vol. 133, June 1933, pp. 695–703.

[127] See also my 'E.H. Carr and the Crisis of Twentieth-Century Liberalism: Reflections and Lessons, *Millennium:* Vol. 38, No. 3, 2010, pp. 1–11.

CHATHAM HOUSE STUDY GROUP

With the progress of time, more and more people have tended to see in national-
ism the root of all our ills. Nationalism(1939)

How critical was soon to become evident as he began work on two separate, but connected studies. Both were begun in late 1936; both were
then published three years later in the autumn of 1939. The research on
one concluded, of course, with the publication of his 'IR' classic *The
Twenty Years' Crisis.* However, while he was researching for the book
which made his reputation as a scholar of international politics, he was also
involved in an extended research project examining the phenomenon of
nationalism. The study, bearing the rather uninspiring title, *Nationalism,*
may have been nowhere near as incendiary as *The Twenty Years' Crisis.* Nor
was it widely reviewed at the time. Nevertheless, it played an important
role for Carr in terms of helping him refine some of his, as yet, unfinished
ideas about the role of the nation-state in the wider international system.[128]

How and why Carr came to be involved in helping produce the
Nationalism volume is in itself an interesting story which tells us much
about the position he now occupied half way between his new role as an
academic holding one of the three Chairs in International Relations in the
United Kingdom and the Think Tank world located then, as now, at the
centre of British power in London. Established in 1920, 'Chatham House',
or as it was more formally referred to, the *Royal Institute of International
Affairs,* was very much a wing of the foreign policy establishment, and
very rarely if ever published anything especially critical of government
policy itself.[129] Naturally enough, as a former Foreign Office 'man', Carr

---

[128] Carr not only chaired the Group throughout its three-year history between late 1936
and 1939, he was also one of the authors of the final Report, along with the historian
Michael Balfour with whom he corresponded regularly throughout. For information on
Balfour see Leonard Miall, 'Obituary: Professor Michael Balfour, *The Independent,* 28
September, 1995. See the archives at Chatham House which contains both the minutes of
the various meetings of the Group, and a good deal of correspondence largely generated by
Carr himself. *Nationalism* finally went to the publishers in July 1939, two months before the
publication of *The Twenty Years' Crisis.*

[129] For a brief history of the Royal Institute see Mary Bone and Charles Carrington, *Chatham
House: Its History and Inhabitants,* London, Royal Institute of International Affairs, 2004.

was very familiar with this world, and it was perhaps no surprise therefore when he was asked by one of the Institute's leading lights—G.M. Gathorne Hardy[130]—to Chair a 'Study Group' tasked with the job of looking at the problem of nationalism in an 'unbiased' and 'scientific' way.[131] The demands of the job were hardly onerous. However, it did involve several meetings in London, constant letter writing to the more active members of the committee, and a good deal of careful editing. Carr in the end was not responsible for all the Group's findings; nor was he its only researcher. Indeed, well over twenty experts submitted evidence, while another six people sat on the committee which he convened. Even so, Carr played a central role throughout, and as the minutes to the many meetings of the Study Group show, he was a very active participant in all its lengthy discussions which in the end led to the publication of a fairly substantial, if somewhat dull volume.[132]

The book began, logically enough, by stating the problem; as Carr put it in a letter to Gathorne-Hardy, the problem was that nationalism which may have been 'desirable in the nineteenth century' was no longer compatible with world order today.[133] But how had this come about? To answer this question the book went into great detail looking in turn at the history of the idea of nationalism, the role played by the French revolution in spreading the new creed, and its transition thereafter from being liberal and democratic in the nineteenth century to becoming anything but in the next. It also dealt with nationalism in all its varieties in several different countries before going on to ask some fairly searching questions about why nationalism had turned out to be 'so vocal and intolerant' in some countries but not in others,[134] why the economic liberalism of the pre-First World War period had now been overtaken by economic nationalism,[135]

---

[130] Geoffrey Malcolm Gathorne-Hardy was one of the first two 'Honorary Secretaries' of the Royal Institute of International Affairs and founding editor of *International Affairs,* the Institute's journal. He wrote, amongst other things, on world politics between the wars, including his popular *A Short History of International Affairs 1920–1939,* Oxford University Press, 1st edition, 1934. Arnold Toynbee claimed that the book was 'the first original contribution the Royal Institute of International Affairs made to the study of international relations'.

[131] *Nationalism,* op cit, p. v.

[132] Jonathan Haslam's dismissal of *Nationalism* with its nearly 350 pages of text as being a 'modest pamphlet' is less than fair. See his *The Vices of Integrity,* op. cit, p. 68.

[133] Quote from Charles Jones, op cit, p. 87.

[134] *Nationalism,* op. cit, p. 189.

[135] Ibid., pp. 217–248.

and what factors more generally had caused nationalism to become increasingly 'baleful and menacing' after the First World War?[136] The Report even addressed issues to which there was never likely to be any answer at all, most obviously what exactly was a nation, how big did a nation have to be before it became viable, was there such a thing as national character, and could multi-nation-states with large minorities function effectively? Indeed, one of the more interesting chapters in the book was the one which dealt very directly with the problem of large multinational states.[137] Here the book left little room for doubt about what had gone wrong in 1919 when it came to reconciling the needs of the new nations with the rights of their minorities. Not only had the machinery which had been set up for sorting out the problem been 'slow and cumbersome';[138] the League itself was then given few powers with which to sanction those 'recalcitrant governments' who had ignored their obligations towards the minorities. Nor were the great powers themselves willing to do much to enforce the rights of minorities. All one could do, it seems, was wait for the brutal march of history—which was becoming increasingly brutal even as the book was being composed—to see what might happen to either the new states themselves or their various minorities.[139]

For a volume that was nearly three years in the making, and which had gathered together some of 'the best and the brightest' in international affairs at the time, its conclusions were, to put it rather mildly, somewhat inconclusive. In part this had to do with the sponsoring institution one of whose guiding ideas was the 'principle of nationality' and the defence of the territorial settlement of 1919; in part too because there was disagreement on the committee itself about whether it was nationalism as such, or the exaggerated form it had taken by the 1930s, that was the problem. Nor was it clear from the volume whether the situation was likely to improve, or whether, as must have seemed obvious by late 1939, it was going to get worse. There seemed to be no consensus either on perhaps the biggest question of all: whether or not the nation-state itself would persist as the unit of power in the international system? There were, it was argued, strong reasons to believe it would survive into the near future. Even so, nothing could or should be ruled out. A world state was unlikely. On the other hand, the international system was for ever changing and the

[136] Ibid., p. xiv.
[137] Ibid., pp. 277–295.
[138] Ibid., p. 292.
[139] Ibid., p. 295.

position of the nation-state in its traditional form could not be guaranteed for ever. It was certainly not beyond the bounds of possibility 'that the political group of the future' would be organized on a different basis than that of territory. In fact, given changes in the world economy and in the character of modern war, there was every chance that larger units would one day become the norm. This would not bring about an end to international conflict as such; the system would remain competitive. However, a very different future seemed to be in the making.

FROM *THE TWENTY YEARS' CRISIS* TO *NATIONALISM AND AFTER*

A world divided between a multiplicity of sovereign states presents difficulties for the creation of world order which have to be frankly recognized.[140]

It is perhaps one of the curiosities of Carr scholarship that his long involvement in a project that went on to inform much of what he later wrote about nationalism and the nation-state only rarely gets a mention in the secondary literature.[141] It is even more curious given that Carr himself later confessed that working on the one (lesser known) volume helped him greatly when it came to composing *The Twenty Years' Crisis* itself.[142] Of course, unlike the study on *Nationalism*, *The Twenty Years' Crisis* has been poured over in painstaking detail by contemporaries and later scholars alike.[143] Whole careers in fact appear to have been constructed trying to work out what Carr really meant, and whether his book was a work of genius or merely the clever scribblings of a man without virtue or morals who couldn't care a jot about whether states were democratic or autocratic, aggressively dangerous or defensive and peace-loving. Yet as more

[140] Quote from E. H. Carr 'The Moral Foundations for World Order' in E.L. Woodward et al., *Foundations for World Order*, Denver, University of Denver Press, 1949, p. 72.

[141] Charles Jones however does provide a useful summary of *Nationalism* in his *E.H. Carr and International Relations*, pp. 85–87.

[142] Carr noted that a number of the 'lines of investigation pursued' through the Nationalism Study Group 'sometimes touched or crossed those' which subsequently appeared in *The Twenty Year's Crisis* (2001 ed., p. cviii, 2016 edition, p. cxxiv).

[143] Carr later referred to *The Twenty Years' Crisis* as 'not exactly a Marxist work but strongly impregnated with Marxist ways of thinking, applied to international affairs'; he added (and this not long before he died) that he became 'a bit ashamed of it' because of its 'harsh realism. Cited in Michael Cox, ed., *E.H. Carr: A Critical Appraisal*, op.cit, p. xix.

sympathetic interpreters of his work have argued, the book works at several different levels and points in many different directions. Thus at one point Carr does argue in what can only be described as brutally realist terms for allowing Hitler's Germany to take over the German-dominated parts of Czechoslovakia, a position for which he was never forgiven by critics. Yet it also contains a clear vision of the future in which the invisible hand of the market and the nation-state are set to play a much diminished role. Carr it is true was not yet prepared to write off the nation-state completely. As he admitted later—rather overstating the point in the process—the original 1st edition of the book published in late 1939 had 'too readily and too complacently' accepted the 'existing nation state—large or small—as the unit of international society'.[144] But there was no doubting where the direction of his thought was now travelling. Nor did there seem much chance of this trend going into reverse. Held up for a while by the First World War and the 'dangerous fiasco' that had been the so-called peace settlement of 1919 with all its nationalist delusions, the 'process of concentration still continued' driven forward by 'technical, industrial and economic developments'. This would not necessarily lead to a single world state as some like H G Wells were advocating at the time. Yet a new kind of international order based on about 'six or seven highly organized units' around which lesser satellite units' would revolve was now very much on the cards.

Nor was Carr alone in thinking that a new kind of international order was required. Confronted with what one writer has termed an 'epochal crisis' without parallel, a whole raft of writers during the 1940s (and even before) were beginning to think about the future in quite radical ways.[145] A few were Marxists or Marxist-influenced like Carr; many more however were liberals who were seeking to rethink Europe and had come to the not illogical conclusion that it was not enough just to defeat Nazism; it was also crucial to mobilize support for the war with visions of a more secure and equitable continent.[146] But it would be a 'new Europe' and not one

[144] E.H. Carr, Preface to the 2nd edition, *The Twenty Years Crisis*, 15 November 1946 (Cox, 2001 edition) p. cvi.

[145] Quote from Or Rosenboim, *The Emergence of Globalism; Visions of World Order in Britain and the United States, 1939–1950*, Princeton University Press, 2017, p. 19.

[146] In Britain one organization which pushed for a new Europe was the Federal Union. Launched in November 1938, by June 1940, it had recruited 12,000 members and had 225 branches throughout the country. It set up the Federal Union Research Institute, chaired by William Beveridge, author of the famous Report of 1942. See Richard Mayne and John

based on old nostrums such as self-determination and sovereignty.[147] These ideas chimed perfectly with what Carr himself had been thinking for some time. Indeed, in a memorandum written to the editor of *The Times* in August 1940, he made clear that it was important to avoid old answers which were not really answers at all. These he insisted had been 'worked to death in 1919' and had only got in the 'way' when it came to thinking rationally about the future of Europe. We should now he went on 'take the line that frontiers and sovereignties' would in the future become 'relatively unimportant'. Instead we needed to focus on the economic reorganization of Europe and the economic and social needs of its people. Equality not liberty, planning not laissez faire, should now be the watchwords going forward.[148]

Carr's forward thinking about Europe perhaps found its fullest expression in his 1942 study *Conditions of Peace*. Here, he not only linked the future of the continent without borders to the idea of economic planning, but went on to insist that there could be no security in Europe unless there was social justice and full employment as well. He also added his own very distinct take on all this by arguing, yet again, that the move towards a new Europe was not just necessary for economic reasons: it was also a natural conclusion to two centuries of historical evolution. Carr also drew lessons from more recent events in Europe, and once more returned to one of his favourite whipping boys: the peace-makers of 1919 and their shambolic efforts to build a new Europe by 'piecing together' various nationalities. This time round though it would be different as new leaders set out to build a 'new Europe' on entirely different foundations which of necessity would require the pooling of resources, an integrated system of transport, and even the establishment of a Bank of Europe all under the direction of a new European Planning Authority. Britain moreover had a very real interest in seeing this new Europe flourish. It itself may not become a fully paid up member of this new project. On the other hand, it

Pinder, *Federal Union: The Pioneers. A History of the Federal Union* St Martin's Press, New York, 1990.

[147] See in particular Peter Wilson, 'The New Europe Debate in Wartime Britain', in Philomena Murray and Paul Rich eds, *Visions of European Unity* Westview Press, A Division of HarperCollins Publishers, 1996, pp. 39–62.

[148] E.H. Carr, 'Memorandum from Mr. Carr to Mr. Barrington Ward', 5 August 1940. Unpublished Manuscript, 8pp. Carr Papers, The University of Birmingham.

would have a very real interest in supporting and underwriting it. Splendid isolation was no longer an option.[149]

Whether it was the optimistic message contained in Carr's *Condition of Peace*, or simply the fact that his ideas were laid out clearly and succinctly, the volume itself turned out to be hugely popular.[150] Many even contrasted its constructive approach to world affairs to what they viewed as having been the rather tough-minded analysis contained in *The Twenty Years' Crisis*.[151] The book certainly seemed to appeal to a wide audience with one American reviewer (in the *Infantry Journal* no less!) calling it 'sensible and thought provoking', another that the book should be 'prescribed' reading for 'every official' in the US government, while a third that 'Professor Carr' (a term Carr always disliked) talked more sense about the future of Europe 'than all the other plans laid from end to end from here to Timbuctoo'![152]

No doubt encouraged by the reception that this particular volume received, Carr clearly thought it worthwhile in synthesizing the various ideas expressed there (and in previous work too) and bringing out a shorter book that would readily appeal to an even wider audience. The result was *Nationalism and After*. Published in 1945, this rather slender volume was in many ways Carr at his very best. Brilliant in execution, dense packed with ideas and argued with a confidence that swept the reader along, the book was another publishing success. Indeed, according to Carr it was much 'better' than the 'pretty feeble' *Conditions of Peace*, even though it contained, like *Conditions of Peace*, 'utopian elements'.[153] Beginning with a succinct restatement of his standard periodization of the nation-state from the progressive nineteenth century and on to what Carr calls the 'third period' when the world witnessed the unfortunate 'infla-

---

[149] Carr it seems was so keen to popularize some of the more detailed arguments advanced in his best-selling *Conditions of Peace* that he published an abbreviated form of the same under the title *The Future of Nations: Independence or Interdependence*, London, Kegan Paul, 1942.

[150] Carr later criticized the *Conditions of Peace* as being a 'terrible example of war-time utopianism that has deservedly been out of print for many years'. See Peter Scott, 'Revolution without the passion', *The Times Higher Education Supplement*, 7th July 1978, p. 7.

[151] For a positive review of *Conditions of Peace*, see C.A.W. Manning, in *International Affairs*, Vol. xviii, No. 5, September-October, 1939, pp. 443–444.

[152] For a sample of the more positive comments about *Conditions of Peace* see the back flyleaf of the US edition of *Nationalism and After*.

[153] Carr made this self-criticism in an autobiographical note composed in 1980. The full version can be found in Michael Cox, *E.H. Carr: A Critical Appraisal*, op. cit, pp. xiii–xxii.

tion of nationalism', Carr took few prisoners as he strode confidently forward swatting away nationalists here and liberal optimists there who together had produced the disaster that was 1919. However, there was, as he had already suggested in *Condition of Peace*, some real cause for hope. Important lessons had been learned and old illusions had been jettisoned. No doubt in Asia the 'demand for self-determination' would still be heard, while 'some of the small units of the past' might continue for a while in Europe. But it was clear that the future would look very different to the past. He stressed (yet again) that this would not lead to the creation of some form of world government or a 'single comprehensive world unit'. On the other hand, there would be far fewer nation-states in a world that was bound to be dominated by a limited number of 'few great multinational units'. This would not necessarily lead to perpetual peace or even to a co-operative world order. But it was the only way forward if Europe and the world was to recover its equilibrium after thirty years of chaos and conflict that had been the hallmarks of the 'age of nationalism'.

THE SOVIET EMPIRE

Thus the new society of the five year plans was a society in which all nationalities were admitted on equal terms, which nevertheless had a distinctively Russian base.[154]

Carr's long journey which had begun in Paris in 1919 was now coming to an end of sorts, and as one door marked 'international relations' began to close another called 'Soviet history' began to open. Planned initially in 1945—just as he was bringing out *Nationalism and After*—little could he, or his publishers have known where this might finally lead and that he would still be in the midst of completing the fifteenth book in the series when he died nearly forty years later. It was by any measure a herculean effort during which he read thousands of original documents, travelled to several archives and consulted with as many sympathetic colleagues as possible when it all seemed to have become too much for him. Of course, the purpose of the exercise which ended controversially before the 1930s began, was not to look in detail at the issue of nationalism as such but

[154] Quoted in E.H. Carr, 'Some notes on Soviet Bashkiria'. E.H. Carr Archives, University of Birmingham.

rather explain how the regime survived its first ordeal by fire (the civil war and intervention), how it then adjusted to the fact that there would be no revolution in the West coming to its aid ('socialism in one country') and why in the end Stalin's 'revolution from above' was an unavoidable necessity.[155]

Yet amidst the millions of words Carr wrote discussing party resolutions, the factional struggles which finally concluded with victory for Stalin, and whether the collectivization of agriculture was a good thing or not—in Carr's view it was—he could hardly avoid looking at one of the very big issues facing the USSR: namely the national question.[156] As Carr soon found out, the revolutionary Lenin, like the liberal democrat Woodrow Wilson, faced not dissimilar challenges when it came to dealing with the consequences of that most appealing but complicated of 'rights' known as the right of self-determination.[157] Moreover, if Wilson had created all sorts of difficulties for the peace-makers in Paris by deploying the slogan, then so too, he felt, had the Bolsheviks when it came to defending the revolution from its many enemies. As he noted in a lengthy discussion in the very first volume of his *History*, though Lenin may have helped the Bolsheviks acquire and then hold on to power by insisting on the right of self-determination-though against much opposition from within the Bolshevik party itself—in practice the idea turned out to be just as much of a problem for the new Soviet Union as it had been for the West. But as Carr also went on to point out, whereas the West had to live with the longer term consequences of Wilson's obsession with nationality, the Bolsheviks managed to 'solve' the problem fairly quickly by the simple device of not following through on its original promise of granting self-determination to all the peoples of the old tsarist empire! He could hardly contain his admiration for the Bolshevik's opportunism. The Soviet leaders had it is true earlier 'raised the cry' of self-determination, but only it seems when it served 'their 'purpose'; and having consolidated their control over a good part (though not all) of the former tsarist Empire, they

[155] See E.H. Carr, 'Revolution from Above', *New Left Review*, November-December 1967, pp. 17–28.

[156] Some of Carr's thinking on Soviet nationalities policy can be found in his 'Dispersal and Reunion' and 'The Bolshevik Doctrine of Self-Determination' Note B, from *The Bolshevik Revolution, 1917–1923* (Macmillan, 1950); Chapter 20 'The Union and the Republics' in *Socialism in One Country* (Macmillan, 1959, Vol. 2); and Chapter 47 'The Soviet State' in *Foundations of a Planned Economy* 1926–1929 (Macmillan, 1971, Vol. 2).

[157] The best source for Carr's thinking on the national question in the USSR is to be found in the 13 files in the Carr Papers, Birmingham University.

soon developed another line. This did not deny the theoretical right of nations to leave the Union. However, it was assumed that their interests would be best served by not exercising the right and remaining within the framework of a 'multi-national state bound together by a tie of loyalty independent of, and indeed opposed to national feeling'.[158]

Carr's preference for the maintenance of the Union over and above the demand for national rights could not have been more clearly expressed. Nothing could be done to prevent secession as in the Baltic republic and Finland; so there was little point in trying to stem the tide. In other parts of the old empire however the situation was much more complex, especially in highly contested regions like the Caucasus and even more so in Ukraine where the working class was small (and largely Russian) and where there was every chance that if the country did achieve full independence it would soon—in Carr's view—ally itself with the capitalist West. Carr was in no doubt where his sympathies lay, and it was certainly not with the West. As he was to argue, one of the many achievements of the early Bolsheviks was not just in thwarting western attempts to destroy the new regime, but in reconstituting 'the territories of the former Tsarist realm' following near complete collapse in 1917. He even compared the success of the Bolsheviks in holding most of the old Russian empire together with the failure of the Ottomans and the Habsburgs. Critics of Bolshevism might have decried the fact: but not Carr. In fact, from the point of view of state formation, Bolshevik policy, brutal though it undoubtedly was, had in this area been a very great success.[159]

Nor did Carr seem to see much that was wrong with the USSR as a Union. Here he was not only expressing his own belief in the Soviet experiment. It also reflected his long held view that large units were always more likely to contribute to global order and economic progress than small ones. Furthermore, like many others of a progressive bent writing during the Cold War, Carr refused to join in what he regarded as the western hue and cry directed against the USSR.[160] This he believed not only smacked of hypocrisy. In its rush to condemn Soviet Union, there was a very real 'danger' that critics would 'pass over in silence its immense

---

[158] E.H. Carr, *The Future of Nations*, op cit, p. 25.

[159] E.H. Carr, 'Soviet Unity and Diversity' *Times Literary Supplement*, June 3, 1955.

[160] One of Carr's collaborators, R.W. Davies, referred to Carr as belonging to the 'anti-Cold War camp' of writers who believed in 'the legitimacy and progressiveness of the Bolshevik revolution'. See his '"Drop the Glass Industry"': Collaborating with E.H. Carr, *New Left Review*, May–June 1984, esp. pp. 59–62.

achievements',[161] including, by implication, its attempts to balance the interests of the centre with the rights of the nationalities. The idea that the USSR had become like old imperial Russia, a 'prison house of nations', would have struck him, and did, as pure propaganda. The Soviet Union had not quite solved its own national question. Nevertheless, the view widespread in some circles in the West during the Cold War that the USSR was only held together by force and intimidation was he believed pure fantasy.[162]

Equally fantastic according to Carr was the idea that self-determination would once again be the answer to the problems facing the countries of Central and Eastern Europe after the Second World War.[163] This may well have chimed with the wishes of his old antagonist the Poles, and no doubt with some Czechs and Hungarians too. But having witnessed the failure of nationalism in Central and Eastern Europe between the wars, Carr was clear that a fundamental reassessment of the region's place within the wider European order had to be found. Indeed, long before the Red Army had achieved victory over Nazi Germany, he had already concluded that small states in general, and not just those in Eastern Europe, could no longer be regarded as being viable. Nor could they ignore the balance of power and the fact that one very formidable power in the form of the USSR now held their fate in its hands. A student of the classics himself, one must also suppose that he was not unaware of the thesis (derived from Thucydides' famous history of the Peloponnesian War) that "the strong do what they will, while the weak suffer what they must."[164] However, he did not need the Greeks to tell him that the age of small independent nation-states had finally passed, and that if they were to survive at all they would only be able to do so by forging what Carr termed a 'permanent alliance' with one of the great powers. This alliance might 'assume the political form of an equal partnership'. But it might not, and in practice

[161] E.H. Carr, 'The Russian Revolution and the West', *New Left Review*, Number 111, September–October 1978, pp. 25–36.

[162] See his 'The Soviet Empire' in *The Times Literary Supplement*, January 27, 1956.

[163] Charles Jones, 'Carr at *The Times*' in Michael Cox ed., *E.H. Carr: A Critical Appraisal*, op.cit, p. 74.

[164] In his 'An Autobigraphy' written in 1980 Carr refers to having studied the Peloponnesian War while an undergraduate at Cambridge and goes on to point out that this had given him 'his first understanding of what history was about'. Quoted in Michal Cox ed., *E.H. Carr: A Critical Appraisal*, op. cit, p. xiv.

the small or 'weak' power would invariably have to 'subordinate its military policy to that of the "strong"'.[165]

Carr's brutal realism when it came to thinking about the fate of what the Americans in particular liked to term the 'captive nations' was hardly designed to win him many friends in the countries of Central Eastern Europe. Yet while his position looks now (as it did to many at the time) to be morally and politically indefensible, not everybody in a position of influence in the West demurred from Carr's hard-headed judgement. After all, hadn't the Second World War sealed the fate of Central and Eastern Europe; moreover, what chance was there of the USSR ever relinquishing control of its newly acquired security blanket?[166] The only question, then, was what degree of control it would seek to exercise, and whether there might be some wider advantage to this new arrangement for the West itself? Indeed, in some western circles—and perhaps in London more than anywhere else—there was a view (not shared by everyone to be sure) that Soviet control over one part of Europe might be a surer foundation on which to build a more stable European order than anything else on offer at the time. If nothing else it would solve the eternal German problem; and it might even keep the USSR tied down for years while recovering from a war that had left it in a quite appalling economic state.[167] Carr also wondered whether what the USSR was doing in Eastern Europe was very much different to what the West itself had done in other parts of the world? After all, hadn't the United States established its own form of hegemony in South America through the instrument of the Monroe Doctrine;[168] and hadn't the British themselves been past masters when it came to exercising control over small nations?[169] Thus why all the outrage, especially as there was every chance that the USSR would now help modernize countries that had for so long been economically marginal? This may not have led to the kind of socialism favoured by pure Marxists; nor did it come without a cost to freedom. However, supported

---

[165] E.H. Carr, *The Future of Nations*, p. 37.

[166] See Graham Ross, 'Foreign Office Attitudes to the Soviet Union, 1941–1945', *Journal of Contemporary History*, Vol. 16, 1981, pp. 521–540.

[167] I have discussed Soviet post-war problems in other places, see in particular Michael Cox, 'Western intelligence, the Soviet threat and NSC-68: a reply to Beatrice Heuser', *Review of International Studies*, Vol. 18, No. 1 January 1992, pp. 75–83.

[168] *The Soviet Impact on the Western World*, op. cit, p. 111.

[169] E.H. Carr, 'Background of Soviet Foreign Policy'. Radio Broadcast, 20 December 1947. Carr Papers, University of Birmingham.

by a younger generation who wished to throw off the shackles of the past, 'a new political order based on a consistent and coherent creed capable of generating devotion and enthusiasm' awaited the states of Central and Eastern Europe. A better, if not a perfect, future beckoned.

CONCLUSION

In this lengthy survey of Carr's evolving views on a complex subject, I have been concerned to provide a detailed understanding of how this rather remarkable writer came to hold the views he did. As I have shown, he was certainly not alone in trying to rethink the position of the nation-state in the international system. Nor was he the only representative of his generation who had arrived at the conclusion that nationalism in its twentieth century form had come to pose both a threat to world peace and an obstacle to international prosperity.[170] Indeed, having been compelled as a young policy-maker to deal with the issue in Paris (an experience that left an indelible mark on his thinking) he continued to reflect on the problem for many years thereafter. The answers he came up with were clearly not to everyone's taste. On the contrary, some of them were hugely controversial, and one can understand why given that he seemed to be indifferent to the fate of small nations, had no hesitation in writing off the Central and Eastern Europe after the Second World War, and had little positive to say about that most basic of international norms: the right of self-determination. Little wonder he had so many critics; the only puzzle is why he didn't have many more!

So how then should we judge his contribution, and what is it we can still learn from Carr apart from a very great deal about the early history of the twentieth century and why it collapsed into chaos between the wars? No doubt Carr got many things wrong from making too enthusiastic a case for appeasement in the 1930s right through to failing almost entirely to develop a critical understanding of the Soviet Union as a system. On the other hand, he clearly got some key things right, and what he most obviously got right—in spite of what some critics have said to the

---

[170] For contemporary critiques of nationalism see George Orwell, 'Notes on Nationalism'. Polemic, No. 1, October 1945. http://seas3.elte.hu/coursematerial/LojkoMiklos/George_Orwell,_Notes_on_Nationalism_(1945).pdf; and Winston Churchill 'Nationalism and Unity'. Churchill's Speech in Holland, 9 May 1946, The Churchill Project, Hillsdale College.

contrary[171]—was that the international system and the position of the
nation-state within it was bound to undergo some fundamental changes
after the Second World War. This did not lead (and he never said it would)
to a new world order based on shared values and norms. He was too much
of a realist for that. Nor did he suggest that world politics might one day
become less conflictual. Yet he was surely correct in predicting enormous
changes in the state system after the Second World War—most obviously
in Western Europe about which he wrote a great deal, but more generally
in the world as a whole. Carr may not have looked forward to a global
'cold war' between the United States and the USSR: at one point he was
even hoping these two 'civilizations' might manage the world together
with Great Britain playing a walk-on part. On the other hand, he did
anticipate a simplified international system in which the great powers
(including the United States about which he later said some rather positive
things)[172] would play a much larger role in international affairs. It is of
course true that a large number of other states did gain independence after
the Second World War. Here though the issue in his mind was not whether
such states could come into being—many had by the 1960s[173]—so much
as how much power and influence they would ever be able to exert in a
deeply unequal world in which they themselves possessed very little by way
of material capabilities.[174] With or without Carr's approval, nationalism in
one form or another would continue to shape the global agenda. But

[171] Even some of Carr's realist admirers in the field of IR still find his work on nationalism
and the nation-state to be puzzling. Carr, according to one wrote 'one of the best books
about international relations' (*The Twenty Years' Crisis*) but then went on to write one of the
'worst' when he brought out *Nationalism and After* in which, we are told, he dismissed
nationalism as a 'passing fad' and predicted a sharp reduction of the number of nation-states
when in fact UN membership after 1945 nearly 'tripled'. See Daniel Drezner, 'The ten worst
books in international relations' *Foreign Policy online*, April 10, 2009.

[172] In a lecture delivered in 1957 to NATO, Carr spoke about the important economic role
played by the United States after the war and its willingness to subsidize 'a considerable part
of the world economy'. See his "Twenty Years' Crisis". Lecture delivered to the NATO
Defense College, 18 July 1957. Unpublished and untitled manuscript. Carr Papers,
University of Birmingham, p. 4.

[173] Carr wrote in 1961 that what 'confronts the politicians and theorists of the mid-twen-
tieth century is the unfamiliar spectacle of unknown groups throughout Asia and Africa arising in their multitude to demand simultaneous recognition as nations and states', See his
anonymous editorial 'What is a Nation?', *The Times Literary Supplement*, July 21, 1961.

[174] See also Robert H. Jackson, *Quasi-States Sovereignty, International Relations and the
Third World*, Cambridge University Press, 1990.

whether the new nation-states that emerged as a result could ever escape the magnetic pull of the more powerful states seemed unlikely.

But what about the relevance of Carr today? Here critics have had something of a field day since his death pointing out that having spent half of his life talking up Soviet achievements, he was hardly in a position to anticipate or foresee the USSR's subsequent collapse. The charge can hardly be disputed. Carr was a product of his times, and like many on the old left he either failed or refused to see the deeper problems eating away at the Soviet system of power. But as Carr might have also pointed out, when empires collapse, as they did after the First World War, it is not necessarily political stability or economic progress that follows in their wake. It did not happen after 1919: and it did not do so again over seventy years later when the end of the Soviet Union initially led to economic chaos, then to a series of small brutal wars (one of which is still going on in Ukraine today), and finally to the elevation of a new strong man in the shape of Putin whose main source of legitimation appears to lie in an ever more extreme form of Russian nationalism. Nor have the states of Eastern Europe found independence from their former overlord to be quite the panacea many thought it would be back in the heady days of 1989. Few but the most rabid of nostalgics would wish to turn the clock of history back. On the other hand, thirty years 'after the fall' many of those who held out such high hopes in their youth are now pointing to the profound challenges now facing nearly all the post-communist states, perhaps the most worrying being a rising tide of chauvinism which is bringing into question the democratic foundations upon which many of these nations were originally founded.[175]

Nor finally has the West itself escaped the contagion of nationalism. The collapse of the communist alternative coming as it did in the midst of an extended period of triumphal capitalist growth seemed to promise a liberal paradise in which markets and democracy would carry all before it.[176] But as Dani Rodrick and Thomas Piketty amongst others warned, the onward march of free market capitalism produced many profound problems including increased inequality and enormous job losses in many of

---

[175] The literature of disillusionment with the velvet revolutions of 1989 continues to grow. See, for example, Ivan Krastev and Stephen Holmes, *The Light That Failed: A Reckoning*, Penguin, Random House, UK, 2019; and Anne Applebaum, *Twilight of Democracy: The Failure of Politics and the Parting of Friends*, Penguin, Random House, UK, 2020.

[176] Ben S. Bernanke, 'The Great Moderation', Remarks at the meetings of the Eastern Economic Association, Washington, DC, February 20, 2004.

the advanced western countries where the balance of economic power had already been shifting decisively away from labour towards capital.[177] Successful in creating wealth for the few, but leaving millions behind in its wake, the whole house of cards finally came tumbling down in 2008. The much debated crisis of the liberal order may have different sources to that which caused the twenty years' crisis between the two wars;[178] and the populist parties which have arisen in the wake of the crash may not be as violent as those extreme parties which arose in the 1930s.[179] Nevertheless, their search for scapegoats, whether it be immigrants or globalization are both symptoms and causes of a new wave of nationalism that is fast threatening the connections that have bound the world together for several decades. Nor does the situation show much sign of improvement in the near future. With China and the United States now locked into a 'new cold war' in the midst of a global pandemic which in itself is fostering suspicion and fear of the 'other', the situation is looking decidedly bleak.[180] History may not be repeating itself. Globalization might be able to survive. The democratic order could endure. Nevertheless, we are clearly at a tipping point moment.[181] A spectre is certainly haunting the world; however, that spectre is no longer communism, as Marx believed it was back in 1848, but rather a rising tide of nationalism and the search for national solutions in a world that still remains highly interdependent. The stakes therefore could not be higher. Long ago Carr warned that we should beware the siren calls of nationalism or thinking we could find answers to the challenges facing humanity through the nation-state. We might be well advised in taking his advice seriously today.

[177] Dani Rodrick, *Has Globalization Gone Too Far?* Washington, DC: Institute for International Economics, *1997;* and Thomas Piketty, *Capital in the Twenty-First Century*, Harvard University Press, 2014.

[178] See, for example, G. John Ikenberry, 'The end of liberal international order', *International Affairs,* Volume 94, no. 1, 2018, pp. 7–23.

[179] For a sample of the rapidly growing literature on populism see Matthew Goodwin and Roger Eatwell, *National Populism: The Revolt Against Liberal Democracy*, London, Pelican Book, 2018; and Francis Fukuyama, *Identity: The Demand for Dignity and the Politics of Resentment*, New York, Farrar, Strauss and Giroux, 2018.

[180] See Umut Ozkirimli, 'Corononationalism', *Open Democracy*, 14 April 2020.

[181] For a balanced assessment see Florian Bieber, 'Is Nationalism on the Rise? Assessing Global Trends', *Ethnopolitics*, Volume 17, Issue 5, 2018, pp. 519–540.

Nationality does not aim either at liberty or prosperity, both of which it sacrifices to the imperative necessity of making the nation the mould and measure of the state. Its course will be marked with material as well as moral ruin. Acton (1862)

CHAPTER 1

The Climax of Nationalism

It is commonly assumed that nations in the modern sense are the product of the disruption of the international—or rather pre-international—order of mediaeval Christendom, and that they represent the projection on a collective national plane of the Renaissance spirit of adventurous and self-assertive individualism. It is further assumed that international relations in the contemporary sense of the term date from the sixteenth and seventeenth centuries, when international wars, recognizably similar to those of more recent times, began to be waged and modern international law first took shape. These assumptions are broadly correct. But the third assumption frequently made that the fundamental character of nations and the type of problem presented by relations between them have remained more or less unchanged through the past three or four centuries is less well founded. The modem history of international relations divides into three partly overlapping periods, marked by widely differing views of the nation as a political entity.[1] The first was terminated by the French Revolution and the Napoleonic wars, having the Congress of Vienna as its tail-piece and swan-song; the second was essentially the product of the French Revolution and, though its foundations were heavily undermined from 1870 onwards, lasted on till the catastrophe of 1914, with the Versailles settlement as its belated epilogue; the third period, whose main features first began to take shape after 1870, reached its culmination between 1914 and 1939. It is still perhaps too soon to say whether we are already passing into a fourth period, as sharply differentiated in character from the third as was the third from its predecessors.

---

[1] The vocabulary of this subject is notoriously full of pitfalls. Since the sixteenth or seventeenth century "nation" with its equivalents in other languages has been the most natural word throughout Western Europe for the major political unit: this explains the paucity of derivatives from the word "state" and its equivalents and the use in their place of words like "national" and "nationalization". The realms of the Habsburgs and Romanovs were, however, not nations but empires; and the colourless legal word "state" covered both them and the nations of Western Europe, as well as the numerous small German and Italian states. In Central and Eastern Europe the word "nation" and its equivalents meant a racial or linguistic group and had no political significance before the nineteenth century, when the doctrine gradually became prevalent that such groups had a right to political independence and statehood ("national self-determination"). In the same way, it has lately become customary to speak of Scottish, Welsh or Indian nationalism, though more rarely of the Scottish, Welsh or Indian nations. The terminology is further complicated by the usage of the United States, where "nation" is reserved for the major unit and "states" are its components and have no international standing; from the American point of view, it would have made nonsense to call the League of Nations a "League of States".

THE FIRST PERIOD

The first period begins with the gradual dissolution of the mediaeval unity of empire and church and the establishment of the national state and the national church. In the new national unit it was normally the secular arm which, relying on the principle *cuius regio, eius religio,* emerged predominant; but there was nothing anomalous in a bishop or prince of the church exercising territorial sovereignty. The essential characteristic of the period was the identification of the nation with the person of the sovereign. Luther regarded "the bishops and princes" as constituting the German nation. Louis XIV thought that the French nation "resided wholly in the person of the King". De Maistre, an early nineteenth-century throw-back to the previous period, argued that the nation consisted of "the ruler and the nobility".[2] International relations were relations between kings and princes; and matrimonial alliances were a regular instrument of diplomacy. The behaviour of the seventeenth- and eighteenth-century sovereigns conformed perfectly to this prescription. The absolute power of the monarch at home might be contested. Even Frederick the Great described himself as the "first servant" of his state. But nobody questioned that in international relations with other monarchs he spoke as one having authority over his "subjects" and "possessions"; and these could be freely disposed of for personal or dynastic reasons. The doctrine of sovereignty made sense so long as this authority remained real and "our sovereign lord the king" had not yet become a ceremonial phrase.

These were the auspices under which international law was born. It was primarily a set of rules governing the mutual relations of individuals in their capacity as rulers, f A treaty was a contract concluded between sovereigns—a form not yet extinct; and the personal good faith of the sovereign was the guarantee of its execution. Grotius in the concluding chapter of *De Jure Belli ac Pads* appealed to "the duty of kings to cherish good faith scrupulously, first for conscience' sake, and then also for the sake of the

---

[2] These and other relevant quotations will be found in F. Hertz, *Nationality in History and Politics,* pp. 274–275, 314, 374. In much of Eastern Europe the restriction of the nation to the upper classes still held good in the nineteenth century. "It was said of a Croat landowner of the nineteenth century that he would sooner have regarded his horse than his peasant as a member of the Croat nation" (*Nationalism, A Report by a Study Group of the Royal Institute of International Affairs,* p. 96). In the middle of the nineteenth century, and even later, the distance which separated the Polish gentry from the Polish-speaking peasantry was still so great that the latter did not as a rule look on themselves as part of the Polish nation.

reputation by which the authority of the royal power is supported". The "international of monarchs", all speaking a common language, owning a common tradition, and conscious of a common interest in maintaining the submissiveness of their subjects, was not wholly a fiction, and secured at any rate formal recognition of a common standard of values. A sense of obligation deriving from the unity of Christendom and the validity of natural law—*rex non debet sub homine, sed sub Deo ac lege,* in Bracton's formula—survived in the secular trappings of the Enlightenment. Claiming the sanctity of law as the basis of their own authority, they could not afford openly and flagrantly to flout it in their relations with one another. It was not a seventeenth- or eighteenth-century autocrat, but a nineteenth-century American democrat, who coined the slogan "My country, right or wrong".

In this scheme of things a common analogy was drawn between the wars of monarchs and the actions at law of private citizens. As Grotius explicitly argues, the causes for which action at law may justly be sustained are those which make it just to wage war. A sovereign waging war no more desired to inflict injury or loss on the subjects of his enemy than a citizen going to law desires to inflict them on the servants of his adversary. They might indeed, and commonly did, suffer from the rapacity and savagery of his pressed or hired soldiers; but his own subjects were also not immune from these hazards. A large part of the early history of international law consists of the building up of rules to protect the property and commerce of non-combatants. Civilians were in effect not parties to the quarrel. The eighteenth century witnessed many wars, but in respect of the freedom and friendliness of intercourse between the educated classes in the principal European countries, with French as a recognized common language, it was the most "international" period of modern history, and civilians could pass to and fro and transact their business freely with one another while their respective sovereigns were at war. The conception of international relations from which these rules and habits proceeded is obviously something quite different from that prevailing in our own time.

Equally characteristic were the national economic policies of the period, to which the name "mercantilism" was afterwards given. The aim of mercantilism, both in its domestic and in its external policies, was not to promote the welfare of the community and its members, but to augment the power of the state, of which the sovereign was the embodiment. Trade was stimulated because it brought wealth to the coffers of the state; and wealth was the source of power, or more specifically of fitness for war. As Colbert, the most famous and consistent exponent of the system, put it, "trade is the source of finance, and finance is the vital nerve of war".[3] Internally, mercantilism sought to break down the economic particularism, the local markets and restrictive regulations, which underlay the uniformity of the mediaeval order, to make the state the economic unit and to assert its undivided authority in matters of trade and manufacture throughout its territory.

Externally, it sought to promote the wealth and therefore the power of the state in relation to other states. Wealth, conceived in its simplest form as bullion, was brought in by exports; and since, in the static conception of society prevailing in this period, export markets were a fixed quantity not susceptible of increase as a whole, the only way for a nation to expand its markets and therefore its wealth was to capture them from some other nation, if necessary by waging a "trade war", War thus became an instrument of mercantilist policy as well as its ultimate end, It is a mistake to contrast mercantilism with laissez-faire as if the one were directed to national, the other to individual, ends. Both were directed to national ends; the difference between them related to a difference in the conception of the nation. Mercantilism was the economic policy of a period which identified the interest of the nation with the interest of its rulers. Its aim, as defined by its most authoritative historian, was "wealth for the nation, but wealth from which the majority of the people must be excluded".[4]

---

[3] Quoted in E. F. Heckscher, *Mercantilism*, ii, 17. The "finance" referred to is public finance.

[4] E. F. Heckscher, *Mercantilism*, ii, 166.

THE SECOND PERIOD

The second period, which issued from the turmoil of the Napoleonic Wars and ended in 1914, is generally accounted the most orderly and enviable of modern international relations. Its success depended on a remarkable series of compromises which made it in some respects the natural heir, in others the antithesis, of the earlier period. Looked at in one way, it succeeded in delicately balancing the forces of "nationalism" and "internationalism"; for it established an international order or framework strong enough to permit of a striking extension and intensification of national feeling without disruption on any wide scale of regular and peaceful international relations. Put in another way, it might be said that, while in the previous period political and economic power had marched hand in hand to build up the national political unit and to substitute a single national economy for a conglomeration of local economies, in the nineteenth century a compromise was struck between political and economic power so that each could develop on its own lines. Politically, therefore, national forces were more and more successful throughout the nineteenth century in asserting the claim of the nation to statehood, whether through a coalescence or through a break-up of existing units. Economically, on the other hand, inter-national forces carried a stage further the process inaugurated in the previous period by transforming a multiplicity of national economies into a single world economy. From yet a third angle the system might be seen as a compromise between the popular and democratic appeal of political nationalism and the esoteric and autocratic management of the international economic mechanism. The collapse of these compromises, and the revelation of the weaknesses and unrealities that lay behind them, marked the concluding stages of the second period. The failure since 1914 to establish any new compromise capable of reconciling the forces of nationalism and internationalism is the essence of the contemporary crisis.

The founder of modem nationalism as it began to take shape in the nineteenth century was Rousseau, who, rejecting the embodiment of the nation in the personal sovereign or the ruling class, boldly identified "nation" and "people"; and this identification became a fundamental principle both of the French and of the American revolutions. It is true that the "people" in this terminology did not mean those who came to be known to a later epoch as the "workers" or the "common people". The Jacobin constitution, which would have substituted manhood suffrage for the substantial property qualification of the National Convention, was never operative.[5] Babeuf went to the guillotine; and the solid and respectable middle class, which made up the "Third Estate", retained through a large part of the nineteenth century a rooted fear and mistrust of the masses. Nevertheless this middle-class nationalism had in it from the first a democratic and potentially popular flavour which was wholly foreign to the eighteenth century. The distance in this respect between Frederick the Great and Napoleon, two ambitious and unscrupulous military conquerors separated in time by less than half a century, is enormous. Frederick the Great still belonged to the age of legitimate monarchy, treated his subjects as instruments of his ambition, despised his native language and culture and regarded Prussia not as a national entity but as his family domain. Napoleon, by posing as the champion and mandatory of the emancipated French nation, made himself the chief missionary of modern nationalism. He was in many senses the first "popular" dictator. Intellectually the transition from Frederick to Napoleon was paralleled by the transition from Gibbon to Burke, or from Goethe and Lessing to Herder and Schiller; the cosmopolitanism of the Enlightenment was replaced by the nationalism of the Romantic movement. The implications of the change were far-reaching. The nation in its new and popular connotation had come to stay. International relations were henceforth to be governed not by the personal interests, ambitions and emotions of the monarch, but by the collective interests, ambitions and emotions of the nation.

The "democratization"[6] of nationalism imparted to it a new and disturbing emotional fervour. With the disappearance of the absolute monarch the personification of the nation became a necessary convenience in international relations and international law. But it was far more than a

---

[5] "The philosophers and political writers of the eighteenth century were unanimously—not excepting Rousseau against the idea of establishing in France a democracy as we understand it the rule of universal suffrage; and the French had been still further encouraged to repudiate the idea of such a democracy by the example of the American English who had established in their republican states a property-owners' suffrage" (A. Aulard, *The French Revolution*, English trans., p. 179).

[6] Here again terminology becomes disputable. The "liberal democracy" or "*bourgeois* democracy" of the nineteenth century is often distinguished from modern "social democracy" or "mass democracy". Some thinkers would regard the restricted democracy of the nineteenth century as liberal but not democratic, and reserve the term democracy for the modern egalitarian form; others would argue that, whereas liberalism is essential to democratic forms of government, socialism has not yet been proved compatible with them.

convenient abstraction. The idea of the personality and character of the nation acquired a profound psychological significance. Writers like Mazzini thought and argued about nations exactly as if they were sublimated individuals. Even today people are still capable, especially in English-speaking countries, of feeling a keen emotional excitement over the rights or wrongs of "Patagonia" or "Ruritania" without the slightest knowledge or understanding of the highly complex entities behind these abstractions. The nineteenth century was passionately devoted to individualism and to democracy as it was then understood; and nationalism seemed a natural corollary of both. What is not so clear is why the rugged individualism of nations should have been regarded as less self-assertive and menacing to peace than the rugged individualism of monarchs, why nations should have been expected to display the princely qualities of forbearance and a sense of honour, but not the equally princely qualities of aggressiveness and greed, why nationalism should have been regarded as a promising stepping-stone to internationalism, and why, finally, it was rarely perceived that nationalism is not so much the apogee of individualism and of democracy as a denial of them. But these questions were seldom asked. A generation reared in the doctrine of a natural harmony of interest between individuals was readily persuaded of a harmony of interest between personified nations. And, after all, the really puzzling question is not why people in the nineteenth century thought as they did, but why, in spite of theoretical arguments which seems so cogent to the present generation, the dynamite of nationalism did not produce its catastrophic explosion for a full century after the downfall of Napoleon, so that this second period of modem international relations looks today like an idyllic interlude between the turbulent first period of warring monarchies and the contemporary, and apparently still more turbulent, period of warring nations.

The first answer would appear to be that the framework of liberal democracy within which nineteenth-century nationalism, at any rate down to 1870, chiefly operated had certain common standards of universal validity which, though different from those of the eighteenth century, were not less effective in upholding a measure of international solidarity. The rights of nations were consciously derived from, and subordinated to, the rights of man which were in their very essence both individual and universal. A nation which did not respect the rights of its own subjects or of other nations denied its own essential character. Moreover, loyalty to this common standard was reinforced by a tangible solidarity of interest. The ruling middle classes who were the bearers of the nineteenth-century nationalism entertained almost everywhere throughout the middle years of the century a lively fear of revolution from below. The rights of property were scarcely less sacrosanct than the rights of man and the functions of the *bourgeois* democratic state—the "night-watchman state" in Lassalle's sarcastic phrase—were largely concerned with its protection. Property, sometimes described as "a stake in the country", was a condition of political rights and—it might be said without much exaggeration—of full membership of the nation: the worker had, in this sense, no fatherland. When Marx appealed to the workers of the world to unite, he was fully conscious of the strength which unity gave to his adversaries. The nineteenth-century *bourgeoisie* of the propertied classes in Western Europe formed a coherent entity, trained to the management both of public and of business affairs (the modern English public school, like the French *lycée*, dates from this period), and united by ties of common ideals and common interests. In their competent hands the democratized nation was still proof for many years to come against the disruptive turbulence of popular nationalism.

The second explanation of the pacific character of the nineteenth-century nationalism goes deeper and is fundamental to the whole nineteenth century. What happened after 1815, though through no particular merit of the peace-makers of Vienna,[7] was nothing less than the gradual development of a new kind of economic order which, by making possible a phenomenal increase of production and population, offered to the newly enfranchised nations of Europe the opportunity to expand and spread their material civilization all over the world, and, by concentrating the direction of this world economic order in one great capital city, created an international—or, more accurately, supra-national—framework strong enough to contain with safety and without serious embarrassment the heady wine of the new nationalism. There was thus a real foundation for the Cobdenite view of international trade as a guarantee of international peace. Not only were the middle-class governments of the western nations united by a common respect for the rights of property and for the principle of non-interference in the management of a world economy which was so triumphantly advancing the wealth and authority of the middle classes, but even Habsburg and Romanov relicts of eighteenth-century autocracy did not disdain the financial crumbs that fell from prosperous *bourgeois* tables and became humble hangers-on of the *bourgeois* economic order.

---

[7] No such windfall awaited the less fortunate peace-makers of Versailles.

This new international economic society was built on the fact of progressive expansion and on the theory of laissez-faire. The expansion of Europe, consisting both in a startling increase in the population and production of Europe itself and in an unprecedentedly rapid dissemination of the population, products and material civilization of Europe throughout other continents, created the fundamental change from the static order and outlook of the eighteenth century to the dynamic order and outlook of the nineteenth century. The initial divergence which explains the whole opposition of principle between mercantilism and laissez-faire is that, while the mercantilists believed that the size of the cake was fixed, the philosophers of laissez-faire believed in a cake whose size could and should be indefinitely extended through the enterprise and inventiveness of individual effort. Restriction and discrimination are the natural reaction of producers to a limitation of demand. In the nineteenth century most people were convinced, on the plausible evidence around them, that a continuously increasing production would be absorbed by a progressively and infinitely expanding demand.

In a world of this kind goods could pass freely from place to place—and not only goods, but men. Freedom of migration was an even more vital factor in the nineteenth-century economic and political system, and more necessary to its survival, than freedom of trade. Newcomers were made welcome by the prospect of their contribution to an expanding production; unlimited opportunity for all who were willing to work was an accepted item in the nineteenth-century creed. The same kind of welcome awaited new nations, whether formed, as in Germany, by a belated application of the mercantilist policy of breaking down internal barriers to unity, or, as in Eastern Europe, by splitting off from former multi-national units. Nations, like individuals, had their contribution to make; and freedom of opportunity should not be denied to them. Human nature being fallible, clashes might no doubt occur. But just as order at home was not threatened by sporadic outbreaks of crime, so occasional wars between the more turbulent nations did not constitute a serious menace to the stability of international society.

The success of this nineteenth-century compromise between a closely knit world economic system and unqualified recognition of the political diversity and independence of nations was rendered possible by two subtle and valuable pieces of make-believe which were largely unconscious and contained sufficient elements of reality to make them plausible. These two salutary illusions were, first, that the world economic system was truly international, and second, that the economic and political systems were entirely separate and operated; independently of each other.

The illusion of the international character of the world economic system rested on the conviction that it was not an artificial creation of man but part of an order of nature. Under absolute laissez-faire all valid economic decisions are assumed to be taken by individuals in the furtherance of their own interest and any central economic authority (or, in present-day terms, planning) to be superfluous, so that the system as a whole remains "impersonal". The nineteenth-century economic order enjoyed its brilliant success largely because people believed that its operation was impersonal and thus in the truest sense international. In fact the hypothetical conditions of absolute laissez-faire did not obtain in the nineteenth-century society, or in any other society which has ever existed. To put the issue in its simplest and most concrete form, progressive expansion was the product not of the principle of universal free trade (which was never applied, and whose application would have been found intolerable) but of the open British market. The colonization of the empty spaces, the development of machine-driven industry dependent on coal and the opening-up of world-wide communications through railways and shipping services proceeded apart under British leadership, and stimulated everywhere the emergence and development of nations and national consciousness; and the counterpart of this "expansion of England" was the free market provided in Britain from the 1840s onward for the natural products, foodstuffs and raw materials of the rest of the world. In recent years it has become customary to dwell on British exports as the foundation of Britain's greatness. It might in most respects be more relevant to stress the significance of her position as the greatest import and *entrepôt* market. The British have in the past been universally regarded first and foremost as a nation of merchants rather than of manufacturers; and beyond doubt the primary foundation of the nineteenth-century economic system was the provision of a single wide-open and apparently insatiable market for all consumable commodities. It was the existence of this national market which made the so-called international system work.

The international system, simple in its conception but infinitely complex in its technique, called into being a delicate and powerful financial machine whose seat was in the city of London. The corollary of an international commodity market was an international discount market, an international market for shipping freights, an international insurance market and, finally, an international capital market. All this required and depended on the effective maintenance of a single international monetary standard into which national currencies were exchangeable at fixed rates; and this in turn presupposed a central control over the currency policies of the different national units, enforced by the potential sanction of a refusal to deal in "unsound" currencies. The prestige of sterling, proudly anchored to the gold standard by the Bank Act of 1844, made it the only serious candidate for the role of international money. The Bank of England, as custodian of the integrity of sterling, found itself—unwillingly and for the most part unwittingly—the final arbiter and court of appeal and the central executive authority of the international system of trade and finance. All gold-standard countries had to keep pace with one another in expanding and contracting the flow of money and trade; and it was the London market which inevitably set the pace. Just as mercantilism in the seventeenth and eighteenth centuries had transformed local economies into a single national economy, so in the nineteenth century the merchants, brokers and bankers of London, acting under the sovereign responsibility of the "old lady of Threadneedle Street", transformed the national economies into a single world economy. It mattered little that they had never sought the function which they discharged, and that they remained unconscious of its scope and importance. The task was thrust on them. "Money will not manage itself", wrote Bagehot in the first chapter of his famous book, "and Lombard Street has a great deal of money to manage."[8] Here was the seat of government of the world economy of the so-called age of laissez-faire.

If then the nineteenth-century system was the work of art rather than of nature, what remains of its international character? No other market could hope to challenge the supremacy of London; and mere supremacy might be held to justify its claims in terms of what would be called nowadays "functional" internationalism. The fetishism of the gold standard made sterling a real international currency. The foreign financier or merchant dealing with, or established in, London enjoyed all the benefits of the system, was treated on his merits and suffered no disability or discrimination. Above all the London market achieved, and deserved, a remarkable reputation for probity and impartiality. It certainly did not seek to serve British interests in any narrow or exclusive sense; the commerce of the world was a British concern. Nevertheless the control exercised from London was continuous; and because it was not consciously directed to

[8] W. Bagehot, *Lombard Street* (concluding words of ch. i.).

anything but the day-to-day task of ensuring the maintenance of sound currency and balanced exchanges—the control which made the whole system work—it was autocratic, without appeal and completely effective. Nor was it, properly speaking, international, much less representative. It was at once supra-national and British.

The second illusion which secured acceptance of the nineteenth-century world order sprang from the formal divorce between political and economic power. The secrecy in which the activities of the city of London were veiled served to mask economic realities from those who thought in traditional political terms; and these activities were altogether withdrawn from political scrutiny. Yet it was precisely because economic authority was silently wielded by a single highly centralized autocracy that political authority could safely be parcelled out in national units, large and small, increasingly subject to democratic control. This economic authority was a political fact of the first importance; and the British economic power of which it was a function was inseparably bound up with the political power conferred by the uncontested supremacy of the British navy. But these interconnexions of political and economic power were overlooked; and since it was not recognized, either by those who exercised the control or by those who submitted to it, how far the political independence of nations was conditioned by the pseudo-international world economic order based on British supremacy, there was no resentment of what would nowadays be regarded as infringements of national sovereignty. Thus, the democratized nations of the nineteenth century went on from strength to strength proclaiming aloud, and exercising in the political sphere, the unrestricted rights of nationalism, while tacitly accepting the discipline of a supreme external arbiter of their economic destinies in the disguise of a law of nature. On this supposed separation of political and economic power, and this real blend of freedom and authority, the nineteenth-century order rested.

In the 1870s the first subterranean rumblings began to shake this splendid edifice. Germany emerged beyond challenge as the leading continental power; and it was in Germany that Friedrich List had sown many years before the first seeds of rebellion against Britain's world economic system. The last imperfect triumphs of free trade were left behind in the 1860s. The German tariff of 1879 was long remembered as the first modern "scientific" tariff—a piece of economic manipulation in the interests of national policy. After 1870 the constructive work of nation-building seemed complete. Nationalism came to be associated with "the Balkans" and with all that that ominous term implied. When British commercial and British naval supremacy were first seriously challenged in the 1890s, ominous cracks soon began to appear in the structure. When this supremacy in both its forms was broken by the First World War, the nineteenth-century economic system collapsed in utter and irretrievable ruin. Subsequent struggles to restore it merely showed how little its essential foundations had been understood.

THE THIRD PERIOD

The third period brings yet another change in the character of the nation. The catastrophic growth of nationalism and bankruptcy of internationalism which were the symptoms of the period can be traced back to their origins in the years after 1870 but reach their full overt development only after 1914. This does not mean that individuals became in this period more outrageously nationalist in sentiment or more unwilling to cooperate with their fellow-men of other nations. It means that nationalism began to operate in a new political and economic environment. The phenomenon cannot be understood without examination of the three main underlying causes which provoked it: the bringing of new social strata within the effective membership of the nation, the visible reunion of economic with political power, and the increase in the number of nations.

The rise of new social strata to full membership of the nation marked the last three decades of the nineteenth century throughout Western and Central Europe. Its landmarks were the development of industry and industrial skills; the rapid expansion in numbers and importance of urban populations; the growth of workers' organizations and of the political consciousness of the workers; the introduction of universal compulsory education; and the extension of the franchise. These changes, while they seemed logical steps in a process inaugurated long before, quickly began to affect the content of national policy in a revolutionary way. The "democratization" of the nation in the earlier part of the century had resulted in the establishment of popular control over the functions of maintaining law and order, guaranteeing the rights of property and, in general, "holding the ring" for the operations of an economic society managed and directed from another centre under rules of its own. The "socialization" of the nation which set in towards the end of the century brought about a far more radical change. Hitherto, as Peterloo and the fate of the Chartists had shown, the masses had had little power to protect themselves against the immense hardships and sufferings which laissez-faire industrialism imposed on them. Henceforth the political power of the masses was directed to improving their own social and economic lot. The primary aim of national policy was no longer merely to maintain order and conduct what was narrowly defined as public business, but to minister to the welfare of members of the nation and to enable them to earn their living. The democratization of the nation in the second period had meant the assertion of the political claims of the dominant middle class. The socialization of the nation for the first time brings the economic claims of the masses into the forefront of the picture. The defence of wages and employment becomes a concern of national, policy and must be asserted, if necessary, against the national policies of other countries; and this in turn gives the worker an intimate practical interest in the policy and power of his nation. The socialization of the nation has as its natural corollary the nationalization of socialism.[9]

The twentieth-century alliance between nationalism and socialism may be traced back to its first—seed in the revolutionary nationalism of the Jacobins; and in France, where the Jacobin tradition remained potent, the Left has asserted itself in successive national crises—in 1871, in 1917 and again in 1940—as the custodian of the national interest' against the compromisers and defeatists of the Right. In its modem form, however, the alliance dates from Bismarck, who, schooled by Lassalle, showed the German workers how much they had to gain from a vigorous and ruthless nationalism—"no sickness insurance without Sedan", as a recent writer has put it.[10] In the same period the word "jingoism" was coined in Great Britain to describe something that had not hitherto existed—the nationalism of the masses; and a decade later it was answered from the other side by Harcourt's famous "we are all socialists now". The successes of Tory democracy, the career of Joseph Chamberlain and the adoption by the Liberal party after 1906 of far-reaching measures of social reform were all straws in the wind. National policy was henceforth founded on the support of the masses; and the counterpart was the loyalty of the masses to a nation which had become the instrument of their collective interests and ambitions.[11]

---

[9] It need hardly be said that the term "national socialism" is not a "Nazi" invention. It seems to have been first used in Germany about 1895 by a group of intellectuals formed by Friedrich Naumann. A few years later it was applied in Austria-Hungary to those Social Democrats who demanded the organization of the party as a federation of "national" units as opposed to those who wished to maintain a single "international" party for the whole of the Habsburg dominions.

[10] F. Borkenau, *Socialism, National or International* (1942), p. 51. This book contains the best critical analysis known to me of the process which I have called "the nationalization of socialism". Its later chapters foreshadowing an organization of Europe west of Russia under Anglo-American leadership bear marks of their date and of a certain anti-Russian bias in the author.

[11] In a work originally published in 1907 the Austrian Social Democrat, Otto Bauer, argued that socialism meant "an increasing differentiation of nations, a sharper emphasis on their peculiarities, a sharper division between their characters", and attacked those who

By the early 1900s, therefore, the breach between the "two nations" had been substantially healed in all the advanced European countries. In the nineteenth century, when the nation belonged to the middle class and the worker had no fatherland, socialism had been international. The crisis of 1914 showed in a flash that, except in backward Russia, this attitude was everywhere obsolete. The mass of workers knew instinctively on which side their bread was buttered; and Lenin was a lone voice proclaiming the defeat of his own country as a socialist aim and crying treason against the "social-chauvinists". International socialism ignominiously collapsed. Lenin's desperate rear-guard action to revive it made sense only in Russia, and there only so long as revolutionary conditions persisted. Once the "workers' state" was effectively established, "socialism in one country" was the logical corollary. The subsequent history of Russia and the tragicomedy of the Communist International are an eloquent tribute to the solidarity of the alliance between nationalism and socialism.

The second underlying cause of the modern inflation of nationalism— its extension from the political to the economic sphere through the reassertion of political power over economic policy—has been everywhere recognized. But it has commonly been attributed to the perversity of politicians or to the nefarious influence of big business, and its far more significant connexion with the socialization of the nation overlooked. The democratic nationalism of our second period had proved manageable and compatible with some kind of international order precisely because its aspirations were predominantly political and could be satisfied within the framework of the nineteenth-century laissez-faire or "night-watchman" state. The social nationalism (or national socialism) of the third period, by shifting the ground from political to economic aspirations, brought about the abdication of the laissez-faire state in favour of the "social service" state. The transition from the predominance of the middle class to the predominance of the masses, or from liberal democracy to mass democracy, was, so far as concerned the nature of the state, the transition from politics to economics. Henceforth the functions of the nation-state were as much economic as political. The j assumption of these functions

believed that socialism would "diminish or even remove the differences between nations" (Otto Bauer, *Die Nationalitätenfrage und die Sozialdemokratie*, 2nd ed. pp. 105–6). Writers on international relations in English-speaking countries had less insight; for the most part they were content to congratulate themselves on the increasing "popular" interest in international affairs and believed that this would promote international concord.

presupposed the abrogation of the international economic order and would, even if there had been no other obstacles, have prevented a revival of that order after 1919. Nationalism had invaded and conquered the economic domain from which the nineteenth century had so cunningly excluded it. The single world economy was replaced by a multiplicity of national economics, each concerned with the well-being of its own members.[12]

The link between "economic nationalism" and the socialization of the nation emerged clearly in the decisive and fateful step taken by all the great industrial countries after 1919—the closing of national frontiers to large-scale immigration. The middle-class governments of the nineteenth century, concerned with the importance of cheap and abundant labour to swell the tide of production and profits, had been under no political compulsion to give prior consideration to the wage levels and standards of living of their own workers; and for fifty years the exclusion of the foreign worker had been the hopeless dream of all labour organizations (it had even preoccupied Marx's First International). Now the prohibition was imposed, contrary to the patent interests of employer and capitalist, almost without opposition[13]; and one of the most effective and necessary safety-valves of the nineteenth-century international order, the avenue of escape opened to the enterprising and the discontented, was closed with a snap. No single measure did more to render a renewal of the clash between nations inevitable. No single measure more clearly exhibited the inherent drive of the new and powerful labour interests towards policies of exclusive nationalism. When in the 1930s humanitarian pressure demanded the admission of alien refugees to Great Britain, consent was given on the condition that they did not "seek employment". The nation was prepared to receive those whose support would be a charge on the national wealth, but not those whose productive capacity might help to increase it.

---

[12] Modern policies of economic nationalism, since they represent a breach with the international order of laissez-faire and are in some respects identical with practices current before the rise of laissez-faire, have sometimes been dubbed "neo-mercantilist". This designation is, however, misleading. From the standpoint of nationalism they constitute not a return to the past, but a further stage in a continuous process of the extension of the nation from the aristocracy to the middle class and from the middle class to the masses.

[13] It should not be forgotten that the attitude of the workers was precisely imitated by the professional middle class in similar conditions. Medical opposition in Great Britain to the immigration of refugee doctors in the 1930s was a conspicuous and not particularly creditable example.

But this was merely one symptom of a far broader trend. Only in Great Britain did the interest of the worker in cheap food keep the labour movement for some time faithful to the free trade tradition; and even here, after 1931, the greater attraction of wage stability won the day. Workers became interested equally with employers in measures of protection and subsidies for industry. Advocacy of such measures proved a fruitful meeting-ground for the hitherto conflicting forces of capital and labour; and national and social policies were welded more firmly than ever together. The same instruments serve both. The "monopoly of foreign trade" and similar organizations elsewhere conform to irreproachably socialist principles; yet they have also proved most efficient instruments of economic nationalism. "Planned economy" is a Janus with a nationalist as well as a socialist face; if its doctrine seems socialist, its pedigree is unimpeachably nationalist. A few years ago "socialism means strength" would have seemed, even to socialists, a paradoxical slogan. Today when a nation determines to exert its utmost strength in war, it resorts without hesitation to policies of out-and-out socialism. Now that laissez-faire has succumbed to the joint onslaught of nationalism and socialism, its two assailants have become in a strange way almost indistinguishable in their aims; and both have become immensely more powerful through the alliance.

The third cause of the inflation of nationalism—the startling increase in the number of nations during our third period—is one of which sufficient account is rarely taken. Here too the year 1870 marks a significant turning-point. Down to that time the influence of nationalism had been to diminish the number of sovereign and independent political units in Europe. In 1871 after the unification of Germany and Italy had been completed there were fourteen; in 1914 there were twenty; in 1924 the number had risen to twenty-six. It would be an understatement to say that the virtual doubling in fifty years of the number of independent European states aggravated in degree the problem of European order. It altered that problem in kind—the more so since the convention ruling in 1871 that only five or at most six Great Powers were concerned in major European issues no longer commanded general acceptance. Nor could the settlement after the First World War be regarded as in any way final or conclusive. National self-determination became a standing invitation to secession. The movement which dismembered Austria-Hungary and created Yugoslavia and Czechoslovakia was bound to be succeeded by movements for the dismemberment of Yugoslavia and Czechoslovakia. Given the premises of nationalism the process was natural and legitimate, and no end could be set to it. After 1914 it spread rapidly to the Arab world, to India, to the Far East; though elsewhere the British Dominions offered the more impressive spectacle of separate nations growing to maturity within the unsevered bonds of the Commonwealth. Moreover, this dispersal of authority occurred at a time when both military and economic developments were forcing on the world a rapid concentration of power: it not only ignored, but defied, a trend deeply rooted in the industrial conditions of the period. The bare fact that there are in Europe today more than twenty, and in the world more than sixty, political units claiming the status of independent sovereign states goes far by itself to explain the aggravation of the evils of nationalism in our third period.

Although, however, this multiplication of national frontiers in Europe and the extension throughout the world of a conception hitherto limited to Western Europe and its direct dependencies have given an immense impetus to "economic nationalism", it may well seem unfair to apply this term in an invidious sense to the natural and legitimate determination of "backward" nations to share in advantages hitherto monopolized by those who had had so long a start in industrial development. The nineteenth-century concentration of industry in a few great countries in Western Europe, which furnished their industrial products to the rest of the world and consumed in return its food and raw materials, may have been a highly practical example of the division of labour. But this privileged status of the industrial nations was self-destructive in so far as it was bound sooner or later to create a desire and capacity for industrial production and a development of national consciousness in the less privileged countries. List had argued as long ago as 1840 that, while free trade might be the interest of industrially mature nations, protective tariffs were a necessary and legitimate instrument for developing backward industries and countries to a state of maturity. In the nineteenth century Germany and the United States had both learned and profited by this lesson. It was now taken up by new and smaller nations all over the world, and the whole machinery of economic nationalism was set in motion to develop their industries and bring them some fraction of the power and prestige which went with industrial development. Such procedures inevitably curtailed international trade and multiplied competition for narrowing markets. The results were disastrous: yet nobody was to blame for them. They arose simply from the multiplication of the number of sovereign and independent nations, each claiming its share in the profits and prerogatives of industrial production.

These three factors—the socialization of the nation, the nationalization of economic policy and the geographical extension of nationalism—have combined to produce the characteristic totalitarian symptoms of our third period. The combination of these factors has found expression in two world wars, or two instalments of the same world war, in a single generation, and has imparted to them a peculiar quality of embittered exasperation for which it would be difficult to find a precedent in any war in history.

THE CLIMAX

The world war of 1914 was the first war between socialized nations and took on for the first time the character of what has since been called "total war". The view of war as the exclusive affair of governments and armies was tacitly abandoned. Before hostilities ended, the obliteration of the traditional line between soldier and civilian had gone very far; attack on civilian morale by propaganda, by mass terrorism, by blockade and by bombing from the air had become a recognized technique of war. Popular national hatreds were for the first time deliberately inflamed as an instrument of policy, and it came to be regarded in many quarters as a legitimate war aim, not merely to defeat the enemy armed forces, but to inflict punishment on members of the enemy nation. In the second world war any valid or useful distinction between armed forces and civilian populations disappeared almost from the outset; both were merely different forms of man-power and woman-power mobilized for different tasks and on different "fronts" in the same struggle. The individual had become little more, in the eyes either of his own national government or of that of the enemy, than a unit in the organized ranks of the nation. In May 1940 an act of Parliament empowered the British Government to make regulations "requiring persons to place themselves, their services and their property at the disposal of His Majesty" for any purpose arising out of the prosecution of the war. Nationalism and socialism joined hands to applaud the most unreservedly totalitarian measure ever adopted by any nation at its hour of greatest need.

The re-establishment of national political authority over the economic system, which was a necessary corollary of the socialization of the nation, was no doubt one of the factors contributing to the situation which produced the two world wars. But it received from them so powerful an impetus that its relation to them is as much one of effect as of cause. The immediate and revolutionary consequence of the outbreak of war in 1914 was the assumption by every belligerent government of the right to create and control its own national money and the deposition of sterling from its role as the universal currency. These measures had their counterpart in commercial policy. The Careful respect extended for more than two centuries to the private property and business interests of the ordinary citizen of a belligerent country was altogether set aside. After 1914 both personal relations and commercial transactions, direct or indirect, with enemy citizens became a criminal offence; and for the first time in the history of modern war enemy private property was confiscated—a devastating blow at the foundations of laissez-faire society and *bourgeois* civilization. International law, framed for days when munitions and military stores were the only contraband and neutrals traded freely with belligerents, was severely strained by submarine warfare on the one side and by an "all-in" blockade on the other. More important still, the change in spirit extended from the methods of war to its purposes. It soon became clear that the terms of peace, whichever side emerged victorious, would constitute an attack on the standard of living of the defeated nation. The kind of policy hitherto reserved for colonial wars against backward peoples was for the first time being turned by European powers against one another. War among socialized nations inevitably became an instrument for securing economic advantages for the victor and inflicting economic disabilities on the defeated. Modern wars are fought to a finish and the loser has no rights.

Nor would it be a legitimate diagnosis which treated these symptoms as the passing aberration of nations at war. In spite of the novel machinery provided by the League of Nations, the period between the wars was marked by a progressive and catastrophic deterioration in international relations, broken only by a brief and uncertain respite between 1924 and 1929. During these twenty years more agreement between nations was recorded on paper, but less substantial agreement attained in practice on major political and economic issues, than at any recent period; nor were acts of aggression confined to those who became the aggressors in the second world war. It would be erroneous to attribute this deterioration to an unhappy accident or to the malevolence of a few men or a few nations; evil men will always be found to turn an unhealthy condition to account. Neither the delegates of fifty or more nations who met at Geneva nor those at home who instructed them were abnormally quarrelsome or abnormally obstinate men. On the contrary their passion for agreement was shown by the pertinacity with which they signed meaningless protocols and resolutions in order to maintain at least the forms of agreement even where the substance was lacking. These men failed to agree precisely because they represented nations in this last and culminating phase of their evolution. In no period 'has there been more talk of cooperation between nations; in few periods less of the reality. As custodians of the living standards, employment and amenities of their whole populations, modern nations are, in virtue of their nature and function, probably less capable than any other groups in modern times of reaching agreement with one another.

The contrast between the comparatively law-abiding habits of members of a national community and the law-breaking proclivities of nation members of the international community has long been a truism; and recent rapid decline in the observance of international law is common ground among all observers. The decline, like the decline in international agreement, is easily explicable in terms of the preceding analysis. The international law of the seventeenth and eighteenth centuries rested on the good faith of sovereigns. What was at stake was the personal execution of personal promises and obligations; and the sense of solidarity among monarchs was sufficient to leave them with a certain desire to keep their word to one another. In the nineteenth century solidarity between middle-class governments, buttressed on respect for the rights of property, and reinforced by fear of offending the international financial authorities in London by any irregularity in the discharge of obligations, still sufficed to keep the observance of international law and agreements on a tolerably high level. Paradoxically enough, it was Bismarck who first diagnosed the symptoms of decline and ascribed it to the unreliability of democracies. The diagnosis was too narrow. The decline was due not to any particular form of government or constitution, but to the socialized nation of which Bismarck was one of the first promoters.

In the contemporary period the discharge of any major international obligation depends on the will of the nation, under whatever form of government, to honour it. An eighteenth-century monarch, operating with foreign mercenaries or with pressed troops drawn from a social class which had no voice in the management of affairs, could undertake to make war in a given contingency with the reasonable assurance that the undertaking could be carried out. In the nineteenth century the rise of liberal democracy led Great Britain to adopt an extremely cautious attitude towards commitments likely to involve anything more serious than a naval demonstration[14]; and the American constitution has up to the present virtually precluded the assumption by the United States of an obligation to make war in any circumstances whatever. In the modern age of the socialized nation and of total war, a prudent government, whatever its constitutional powers, may well doubt its competence to give such an undertaking—at

---

[14] It is worth recalling the three classic pronouncements on the subject: Castlereagh's State Paper of May 5, 1820; Gladstone's refusal in the House of Commons on August 10, 1870, to treat the Belgian guarantee treaty as a "rigid" obligation; and Salisbury's memorandum of May 29, 1901.

any rate for more than a few days or weeks ahead; and this caution applies in particular to unspecified obligations like those in the Covenant of the League of Nations. Even the policing of conquered enemy territory with conscript armies is an obligation which no modern democracy can lightly assume for any prolonged period.

Financial and economic commitments are equally suspect. They may be accepted by governments in all good faith, but without full understanding of their consequences; and should these eventually turn out to be detrimental to the standard of living or level of employment in one of the contracting countries, they will be dishonoured, as Great Britain dishonoured her financial obligations to the United States in 1933.[15] Nor can the general provisions of international law be any longer observed by a modem nation if their observance is found or believed to involve loss of life or risk of defeat in time of war, or serious economic loss in time of peace. The first obligation of the modern national government, which no other obligation will be allowed to override, is to its own people. It would be absurd to lament this state of affairs as proof of increased human wickedness; it might equally well be regarded as proof of a sharpened social conscience. But whatever view we take of it, it would be folly to neglect the overwhelming evidence that modern national governments cannot and will not observe international treaties or rules of international law when these become burdensome or dangerous to the welfare or security of their own nation. Any so-called international order built on contingent obligations assumed by national governments is an affair of lath and plaster and will crumble into dust as soon as pressure is placed upon it. In peace, as in war, the international law of the age of sovereigns is incompatible with the socialized nation. The failure to create an international community of nations on the basis of international treaties and international law marks the final bankruptcy of nationalism in the west.

---

[15] The *locus classicus* on the subject is the statement made by the then Chancellor of the Exchequer, Neville Chamberlain, on the occasion of the last full payment made by Great Britain under the American war debt agreement: "When we are told that contracts must be kept sacred, and that we must on no account depart from the obligations which we have undertaken, it must not be forgotten that we have other obligations and responsibilities, obligations not only to our own countrymen but to many millions of human beings throughout the world, whose happiness or misery may depend upon how far the fulfilment of these obligations is insisted upon on the one side and met on the other" (*House of Commons Official Report*, December 14, 1932, vol. 273, col. 354).

Meanwhile the extension of the geographical limits of nationalism has meant not only a multiplication of the number of nations, but a planting of nationalism in new and unfamiliar soils. In Western Europe nationalism had grown in soils fertilized by the traditions of Christendom, of natural law and of secular individualism. In German lands the natural law and individualist traditions had struck only light roots; in Russia and other countries dominated by the Orthodox Church they had been ignored or rejected. Beyond Europe nationalism was now spreading to countries where every Christian or European tradition was alien, and where the illogical inhibitions which had for so long helped to restrain European nationalism were unknown. Even in Europe the ruthlessness of the First World War did much to break down these inhibitions. The Second World War was started by a German power which scarcely paid even lip-service either to the humanitarian tradition of individualism or to the universalist tradition of natural law. Mass deportations of civilians have been carried on all over Europe; in Eastern Europe a large number of Jews have been deliberately exterminated. Germany in several cases, and Japan in the notorious attack on Pearl Harbour, took military action without any previous declaration of war. International law had come to seem almost irrelevant except perhaps when it could be invoked to discredit an opponent. In the conduct of the war there have been gradations of inhumanity and ruthlessness, significantly corresponding to the degree in which the respective theatres of war had participated in the Western European tradition. It has been fought with greater ferocity in Eastern than in Western Europe, and with most savagery of all in Asia and the Pacific. Neither Russia nor Japan is a party to the Geneva Convention on prisoners of war; and in Germany powerful and specifically Nazi organs showed an increasing disregard for its obligations.

Yet it would be premature to claim for Western Europe any exemption even from the worst brutalities of international strife. The collapse of military discipline and the release of the conquered countries from four years of grinding oppression may yet lead to outbreaks which will match in horror anything that has occurred in other parts of the world. Nor is there much in declared national policies which holds out hope of an ultimate pacification between nations. Perhaps the apex of nationalism is reached when it comes to be regarded as an enlightened policy to remove men, women and children forcibly from their homes and transfer them from place to place in order to create homogeneous national units. Such plans were first canvassed in the first flush of French revolutionary nationalism when the Jacobins wished to deport the German-speaking population of Alsace arid replace it with good Frenchmen.[16] Having remained dormant for a 125 years, they revived after the First World War. In January 1919 Venizelos was already proposing to tidy up national frontiers in Asia Minor by "a wholesale and mutual transfer of population"; and about the same time Mackinder in his famous essay in geopolitics suggested an exchange of the German population of East Prussia for the Polish population of Posen.[17] Minor transfers of population were subsequently carried out between Turkey and Greece and Greece and Bulgaria; and these desperate expedients were unhappily invested by the League of Nations with a spurious and untimely air of high-mindedness, which was apparently not dispersed even when Hitler drew liberally on the precedent thus created. Today annexations of territory are regarded as more, not less, respectable if they are accompanied by wholesale deportation of the existing population—not perhaps the most callous act recorded in history, but surely the most explicit exaltation of the nation over the individual as an end in itself, the mass sacrifice of human beings to the idol of nationalism.

---

[16] Authorities quoted in F. Hertz, *Nationality in History and Politics*, p. 86.
[17] H. Mackinder, *Democratic Ideals and Reality* (Pelican, ed., 1944), p. 121.

A FOURTH PERIOD?

The Second World War thus marks the climax and the catastrophe of the third period of modern international relations, and leaves us on the threshold of a fourth period whose character will probably shape the destinies of mankind for a century to come. A first view suggests beyond doubt that nationalism has never been stronger than at this moment; and this view would lead to almost unqualified pessimism about the future of international relations. Yet closer analysis may reveal certain trends, not necessarily more reassuring, but at any rate sufficiently different to suggest that, whatever may be in store in the next few years, nations and international relations are in process of undergoing another subtle, not yet clearly definable, change.

Paradoxically enough, certain features of the war itself seem to mark a retrogression from the unqualified nationalism of the preceding period. The absence of any trace of national exaltation or enthusiasm on the outbreak of the Second World War offered in all countries—and not least in Germany itself—a striking contrast, which was much remarked at the time, to the patriotic fervour of 1914. National hatreds have lost their old spontaneous frankness, and mask themselves delicately in ideological trappings. In Germany the "hymn of hate" has not reappeared; in Great Britain what is called "Vansittartism" is the rather shamefaced rationalization of a frank popular emotion of the last war. Even the "nationalism" of Hitler became, as time went on, less and less specifically German. It was "Aryan" or "Nordic"; and, driven first by the needs of *Grossraummrtschaft* and later by the demand for manpower, it began to discover these attributes in unexpected places. Full and impartial information of the extent and significance of "quislingism" in many countries can hardly be expected for some time. It was perhaps not surprising that it should have infected newly created national units like Czechoslovakia and Yugoslavia; but widespread "collaboration" in the European country with the oldest and most deeply rooted national tradition of all was a new and startling development. Ten or 12 million foreign workers in German factories, factories in occupied countries working under high pressure on war production, substantial contingents of a dozen foreign nationalities embodied in the German armies, the extensive recruitment of foreigners not only for the rank and file, but for the officer corps, of the crack and highly trusted *Waffen S. S.*—these phenomena are not wholly explicable in terms of brute force, and seem difficult to reconcile with the picture of an age of unbridled and militant nationalism. Political warfare, whose contribution to Hitler's victories in 1940 and 1941 can hardly be denied, is at once a symptom and a cause of the decline of nationalism. It succeeds only by finding rifts in national solidarity; it aims at widening and deepening those rifts. Some plausibility must be accorded to a shrewd comment penned at the peak of German power in Europe that "Hitler's successes are basically rooted, not in his extreme nationalism, but on the contrary in his shrewd judgment of the decay of nationalism among his neighbours".[18]

These casual pointers might be dismissed as misleading and exceptional if they did not seem to coincide with other and broader indications. As the Second World War draws to a close, none of the main forces that have gone to make the victory is nationalist in the older sense. Neither Great Britain nor the British Commonwealth was ever finally engulfed in the nationalist tide. The word "British" has never acquired a strictly national connotation; and there is no name for the citizen of the entity officially known as "the United Kingdom of Great Britain and Northern Ireland". More significant are the non-national names and multi-national status of the two new giants of world politics—the United States and the Soviet Union. It is the pride of the United States to have been the "melting-pot" of nations. In the American army for the liberation of Europe men of German, Polish, Italian, Croat and a dozen other national origins have marched side by side; in the presidential election of 1940 one candidate could speak with pride of his Dutch, the other of his German, ancestry. In the Soviet Union a fluctuating attitude towards the national issue has ended, under a Georgian leader, in the emphatic promulgation of a comprehensive Soviet allegiance which embraces in its overriding loyalty a multiplicity of component nations.

The climate at the end of the Second World War will therefore be very different from that of 1919 when the disruption of the Habsburg, Romanov and Turkish empires under the banner of national self-determination was regarded as a landmark of progress in international relations. This may well turn out to have been the last triumph of the old fissiparous nationalism, of the ideology of the small nation as the ultimate political and economic unit; for it was one of those victories which prove self-destructive to the victor. Political changes, whether evolutionary or revolutionary, rarely make themselves felt everywhere with equal intensity or at the same rate of advance. In Asia the demand for self-determination

[18] F. Borkenau, *Socialism, National or International* (1942), p. 165.

may still be heard, though perhaps more faintly and less confidently than of late. In Europe some of the small units of the past may continue for a few generations longer to eke out a precariously independent existence; others may retain the shadow of independence when the reality has disappeared. But their military and economic insecurity has been demonstrated beyond recall. They can survive only as an anomaly and an anachronism in a world which has moved on to the other forms of organization. But it remains to consider what these forms may be, and whether there is any hope of making them more tolerable to mankind than the forms of the recent past.

CHAPTER 2

The Prospects of Internationalism

The contemporary challenge to the nation as the final and acceptable unit of international organization comes on two fronts—from within and from without, from the standpoint of idealism and from the standpoint of power. On the plane of morality, it is under attack from those who denounce its inherently totalitarian implications and proclaim that any international authority worth the name must interest itself in the rights and well-being not of nations but of men and women. On the plane of power, it is being sapped by modem technological developments which have made the nation obsolescent as the unit of military and economic organization and are rapidly concentrating effective decision and control in the hands of great multi-national units. The two attacks are not wholly independent of each other; for it is the failure of the nation-state to assure military security or economic well-being which has in part inspired the widespread questioning of the moral credentials of nationalism. The future depends on the strength of each, and on the nature of the balance which may be struck between them. The challenge from within may be considered first.

E.H. Carr, *Nationalism and After*,
https://doi.org/10.1057/978-1-349-96038-5_2

INDIVIDUAL AND NATION

Every established historical institution acquires vested interests and stakes out for itself claims which must from time to time, and especially in periods of crisis, be submitted anew to the test of first principles. The challenge to nationalism does not exclude recognition of the place of nations in an international order; it clears the way for a better understanding of what that place is. The nation is not a "natural" or "biological" group—in the sense, for example, of the family. It has no "natural" rights in the sense that the individual can be said to have natural rights. The nation is not a definable and clearly recognizable entity; nor is it universal. It is confined to certain periods of history and to certain parts of the world. Today—in the most nation-conscious of all epochs—it would still probably be fair to say that a large numerical majority of the population of the world feel no allegiance to any nation. Nevertheless the nation is something far more than a voluntary association; and it embodies in itself, though overlaid with conventional trappings, such natural and universal elements as attachment to one's native land and speech and a sense of wider kinship than that of family. The modern nation is a historical group. It has its place and function in a wider society, and its claims cannot be denied or ignored. But they can in no circumstances be absolute, being governed by historical conditions of time and place; and they have to be considered at the present moment primarily in relation to the needs both of security and of economic well-being. What has to be challenged and rejected is the claim of nationalism to make the nation the sole rightful sovereign repository of political power and the ultimate constituent unit of world organization—a claim gradually asserted over the past three centuries, though not finally conceded, and then only for the European continent, till 1919.

It is a fundamental tenet of nationalism that any international order must take the form of an association of nations—that, just as the national community is composed of individual members, so the international community must be made up of nation members. In the first period of international relations reviewed in the previous chapter this assumption had been natural enough; the members of the international community were individual sovereigns. In the second period the personified nation had taken the place of the person of the sovereign. The assumption of the previous period was beginning to wear a little thin. But the survival of monarchy in all the principal countries helped to keep it in being. The concert of Europe was originally conceived as a conclave of monarchs or their personal agents; and periodical meetings between sovereigns continued to be a significant part of its machinery. In the third period even this myth of an international conclave of rulers was dead, though one faint attempt was made to revive it in a democratic guise through the publicity given to the largely imaginary personal character of relations between Austen Chamberlain, Briand and Stresemann. But the myth had by this time obtained so strong a hold that the substitution of corporate nation for individual ruler was for the most part quite unconscious. Few people in the period between the two wars doubted that the international community must be composed of nations or were specifically aware that this enormous assumption was being made.

The supposed analogy between a national community of individuals and an international community of nations, which was the stock-in-trade of much international oratory between the two wars, requires us to believe that the members of the international community, like the individuals composing a national community, are known, recognizable and comparable entities. This assumption is open to question. The sovereigns who formed the international community of the seventeenth and eighteenth centuries were members in virtue of their power; the effective test was that of might. The same held good of the Great Powers forming the nineteenth-century concert of Europe. But the European settlement of 1919 was based on the admission of two new and revolutionary claims—the claim of racial and linguistic groups to political independence and statehood in virtue of their quality as nations, and the claim of all independent states to effective membership of the international community. Membership of the international community thus became ostensibly a matter not of might but of right. In theory this seemed to mark an immense progress. In practice it proved impossible to discover any distinguishing marks by which the right of a self-styled nation to statehood could be objectively determined, or to exclude either the criterion of might or the criterion of political expediency, so that membership of the international community became itself a subject of uncertainty and dispute. Once it was proclaimed that nations, like individual human beings, were independent and self-determined entities, the question inevitably arose, What nations? And to this question there was no determinate answer.

The difficulty became far graver when political thinkers, pursuing the analogy of the individual, began to ascribe to nations natural rights such as freedom and equality. The nineteenth century recognized the freedom of nations as a corollary of democracy; and few thinkers either in the nineteenth century or between the two wars appear to have enquired into its precise meaning or validity. Yet freedom is a prerogative of the individual man and woman: it is only by a conventional metaphor, which easily becomes a *cliché* and is sometimes barely distinguishable from the Hitlerian exaltation of the nation as an object of worship and an end in itself, that freedom is attributed to nations. Freedom for a nation has meaning in so far as it is demanded by the men and women who make up the nation and felt by them as essential to their freedom. But national freedom which opens the way, as it did in some countries between the two wars, for the consistent denial of elementary rights and liberties to large sections of the nation is little better than a contradiction in terms. It is well known that a good many people in central Europe after 1919 regretted the national freedom which had liberated them from the Habsburg empire. The assumption that ordinary men and women gladly accept loss of their means of livelihood or of their personal liberties as the price of the freedom of their nation will be readily made only by those who have not suffered the experience.

The same conclusion is equally valid for another right conventionally coupled with freedom—the right of equality. It is a commonplace that no political community can be established among individuals divided by conspicuous, significant and irremediable inequalities. Within the political unit this difficulty has usually been solved by including in the effective community only members of the most powerful group—white men, landowners, propertied classes and so forth—between whom some measure of equality exists; internationally this was the solution which in the nineteenth century gave some reality to an international community of Great Powers. This exclusive solution is no longer acceptable. But its rejection confronts the world with the impossible task of creating an international community out of units so fantastically disparate (leaving out of account the three predominant powers) as China and Albania, Norway and Brazil.[1] The reference in the draft Charter of the United Nations prepared at Dumbarton Oaks to "the sovereign equality of all peace-loving states" must be regarded as evidence either of a high degree of political simplicity

---

[1] For a discussion of the absence of equality as a fundamental flaw in the international community, see E. H. Carr, *The Twenty Years' Crisis* (1939), pp. 206–10. The conclusion there recorded is that "the constant intrusion, or potential intrusion, of power renders almost meaningless any conception of equality between members of the international community". At that time I still believed in the possibility of achieving a community of nations: it now seems to me clear that this belief must be abandoned.

or of a scarcely less discouraging readiness to pander to popular superstition. Like the right of freedom, the right of equality, however interpreted and conditioned, is one that can be attributed only to individuals, not to nations. What we are concerned to bring about is not the putting of Albania on an equal footing with China and Brazil, but the putting of the individual Albanian on an equal footing, in respect of personal rights and opportunities, with the individual Chinese or the individual Brazilian. The equality of nations is not only unattainable, but is neither equitable nor desirable. The equality of individual men and women is not indeed wholly attainable; but it is an ideal which, at any rate in some of its connotations, can be accepted as a constant aim of human endeavour.

The challenge to the socialized nationalism of our third period thus issues in a protest against an international order which accepts as its basis the submersion of the rights of the individual in the rights of the nation. The international order of the future cannot be a society of free and equal nations bound together by a constitutional system of mutual rights and obligations. The freedom and equality which the makers of the coming peace must seek to establish is not a freedom and equality of nations, but a freedom and equality which will express themselves in the daily lives of men and women. It would not be difficult to detect, even before the outbreak of the Second World War, symptoms of a growing consciousness of this need. The so-called technical organs of the League of Nations, including the International Labour Organization, imperfect though they were, displayed a far greater vitality than the political organs; and it is significant that they were concerned with matters directly affecting the welfare of individuals rather than the security of nations. A similar evolution may perhaps rescue international law from the disarray into which it has fallen. A recent critic has distinguished "two strains" in modern international law:

One has been concerned with the relations between states as such ... the other has used international law for promoting and protecting, through international cooperation and institutions, the interests and welfare of the individual.[2]

The driving force behind any future international order must be a belief, however expressed, in the value of individual human beings irrespective of national affinities or allegiance and in a common and mutual obligation to promote their well-being.

---

[2] H. Lauterpacht, *The Law of Nations, the Law of Nature and the Rights of Man* (Grotius Society, 1944), p. 27.

On the other hand the demonstrable bankruptcy of nationalism, political and economic, must not be used to justify a plunge into the visionary solution of a supreme world directorate. The plea for the emancipation of the individual must not be interpreted as a plea for a sentimental and empty universalism. The sense of the unity of mankind, sufficient to support the common affirmation of certain universal principles and purposes, is not yet strong enough, according to all available evidence, to sustain an organization exercising a sovereign and universal authority. Popular slogans like Wendell Willkie's "one world" are misleading. To reduce the time of transit between two capitals from weeks to days, or from days to hours, provides no assurance, at any rate in the short run, of a growth of mutual understanding and united action. Notwithstanding the vast improvement in communications, indeed, the world may be less "one" today than it was in the nineteenth century when Great Britain enjoyed a greater ascendancy than had been exercised from any single centre since the heyday of the Roman Empire. The contemporary world gravitates towards several competing centres of power; and the very complexity of modern life makes for division. The lure of universality has had since 1919 a dangerous fascination for promoters of international order. The universality of any world organization almost inevitably tends to weaken its appeal to particular loyalties and particular interests. It was probably a weakness of the League of Nations that its commitments were general and anonymous: it imposed the same obligations on Albania as on Great Britain, and the same obligation on both to defend the independence of Belgium against Germany and that of Panama against the United States. These generalities could be justified in terms of pure reason but not translated into terms of concrete policy, so that the whole structure remained abstract and unreal, The history of the League of Nations, beginning with the insertion in the Covenant of the original Monroe Doctrine reservation, bears witness to the persistence of attempts to escape from a theoretical and ineffective universalism into a practical and workable regionalism. A world organization may be a necessary convenience as well as a valuable symbol. But the intermediate unit is more likely to be the operative factor in the transition from nationalism to internationalism.

The same caution must be applied to schemes of worldwide economic organization. The protest against nationalism will certainly not find expression in a return to the aristocratic cosmopolitanism of the Enlightenment or to the laissez-faire individualism of the nineteenth century. The socialized nation of our third period cannot be spirited out of existence. The mercantilism which stood for "wealth for the nation, but wealth from which the majority of the nation must be excluded" is dead. But the laissez-faire individualism which purported to interpose no effective economic unit between the individual at one end of the scale and the whole world at the other is equally gone beyond recall. The pursuit of "free competition", of an economic principle of all against all, inevitably tends to create those extreme inequalities and forms of exploitation which offend the social conscience and drive the less privileged to measures of self-defence, which in turn provoke corresponding countermeasures. By the end of the nineteenth century this process had led, as it was bound to lead, to the progressive development of combination at every level and in every part of the system, culminating after 1914 in the most powerful combination yet achieved—the modern socialized nation. Thus measures of national self-sufficiency and economic nationalism which seem to negate free competition are in another aspect its natural consequence. But a further stage has now been reached. What was created by a cumulative process of combination between individuals to protect themselves against the devastating consequences of unfettered economic individualism has become in its turn a threat to the security and well-being of the individual, and is itself subject to a new challenge and new process of change.

Yet it is abundantly clear that this change cannot consist in any mere reversal of existing trends. The explicit or implicit undertone of much current discussion encourages the belief that the whole course of economic evolution in the twentieth century is an error to be retrieved by returning to the universalism of an idealized past. Such a view, which inspired a long series of abortive international conferences from Brussels in 1920 to Bretton Woods in 1944, is both false and sterile. The forces which produced the socialized nation are still operative; nor will its demands be abated. Indeed the fact that these demands can no longer be met within the national unit, and that the same forces are now at work to break its bounds, is perhaps the best hope for the development of an international system in our fourth period. The just criticism of the economic nationalism of the period between the two wars should be directed not so much against the methods it has used—though some of them were merely restrictive and aggressive, others were the intelligent and necessary instruments of a first, faltering attempt to plan international trade—as against the narrowness and inappropriateness of the geographical limits within which these methods were employed. It was not that intermediate units of economic organization were not required, but that nations had ceased to be convenient, or even tolerable, units for this purpose. The answer to the socially and internationally disruptive tendencies inherent in the juxtaposition of a multitude of planned national economies is not an abandonment of planning, but a reinforcement of national by multi-national and international planning.

Recognition of the inadequacy of the national unit on the one hand and of a single comprehensive world unit on the other leads to the question of the shape and size of the requisite intermediate units of organization. Ideally this should beyond question be determined by the end in view. Different units are appropriate for different purposes—an international authority for rail or road transport will not cover the same area as an international authority for air transport. Different units are appropriate for the same purpose at different periods—one of the cardinal international problems of today is that what might have been workable economic or military units in the eighteenth and nineteenth centuries have become impracticable in the light of modern conditions of industrial production or military technique. Hence the scope and constitution of different authorities must, on severely practical grounds, be determined according to the purposes which they are required to serve, on the principle of what has come to be called "functional" instead of national organization. Even before 1914 there were, among other examples, two international commissions controlling navigation on different sectors of the Danube, an international railway union for Europe, and a Latin monetary union. Between the two wars the technical organs of the League of Nations, though sometimes hampered by a fictitious universalism, and sometimes by the absence for irrelevant political reasons of members who could have contributed effectively to their work, did good service; in the 1930s international commodity controls became for the first time a salient feature in world economic organization. During the Second World War a vast number of new functional international organizations have been created. Some of them fulfil purposes which will end with the war; others like those which control and allocate essential raw materials, food and shipping may well be carried on into the period of peace. Among the most remarkable of all these creations has been the Middle East Supply Centre which, starting as a clearing-house for the scanty supplies available for the civilian populations of the Middle East in the war crisis of 1940–1941, has come to play a vital role in developing the economic life of some fourteen countries. Bodies like Unrra and the Food and Agriculture Organization established by the Hot Springs conference of 1943, which look forward to the period after hostilities, have been conceived on a universal basis. Nevertheless it is already clear that they will be effective only in so far as they create separate organs for specific purposes in different areas.

These organizations have certain common qualities which explain both their value and the resistance likely to be encountered by them. In the first place, they are international in the sense that, while they operate on national territories with the tacit or explicit consent of the national governments concerned, they are not organs of these governments and do not formally derive authority from them. Secondly, they are international not in the sense that they exercise any authority over national governments, but in the sense that they operate in a number of countries without regard to the divisions and distinctions between them. Thirdly, the nature of their authority is "non-political in that it does not ostensibly affect the sovereign powers vested in the national governments. In all these respects they constitute a striking parallel with the financial and economic 'system of the 19th century, operated all over the world by the organs of an anonymous authority having' no precisely defined status, but enjoying in virtue of its 'non-political'" services and its prestige the toleration and approval of the national governments. Nor should another parallel be overlooked. It would be simple today—as it would have been simple in the nineteenth century if anyone had thought it worthwhile—to point to the fictitious elements in the separation of non-political from political authority, and to demonstrate that political power, however disguised and diffused, is a presupposition that lies behind any authority, however non-political in name. Nevertheless the world today, like the world of the nineteenth century, may have to put up with a certain salutary make-believe if it can find no way of consciously and deliberately effecting an international separation of powers. In the national community the concentration of all authority in a single central organ means an intolerable and unmitigated totalitarianism: local loyalties, as well as loyalties to institutions, professions and groups must find their place in any healthy society. The international community if it is to flourish must admit something of the same multiplicity of authorities and diversity of loyalties.

The view of an eventual world union to which the, application of these principles would lead has been set forth by a recent American writer in terms which cannot be bettered:

> Let us not, then, irritate national egoism or offend the pride of sovereignty by inaugurating the union with flourish of trumpets, impressive ceremonies,

and pledges given and taken for all future time. All of the words, resolutions, pledges, binding treaties, and solemn covenants that might conceivably induce the nations of the world to cooperate for the creation of a new and better world were uttered after the last war. What is needed is something less edifying and more prosaic, something less noisy but more effective. The contemplated union, league, federation, or whatever it is to be, will have a better chance of success if it begins, so to speak, "unbeknownst to itself", if it begins without declaring, or even professing to know, what nations may ultimately belong to it, or what the precise rights and obligations of its members may turn out to be. It will have a better chance of success, in short, if it begins with the drafting of specific agreements between a few or many nations for dealing with specific problems, and the creation of whatever international commissions, boards, agencies, may seem best suited to dealing with the specific problem in hand. ... Such a union would be less in the nature of a created mechanism than a developing organism. It would at any time be what it could be effectively used for doing, and would ultimately become, in form and procedure, what seemed best suited to accomplishing the ends desired—the promotion of the common interests of its members and the preservation of amity and peace among them. In so far as such a union succeeded in accomplishing these ends, it would imperceptibly acquire "power", and as it acquired power, nationalism would no doubt be imperceptibly abated and the independence of sovereign states imperceptibly curbed.[3]

It must, however, be admitted that this idealistic view of a functional internationalism, based on the conception of international order as association not between nations as such but between people and groups of different nations, and realized through an indefinite number of organizations cutting across national divisions and exercising authority for specific and limited purposes over individuals and functional groups, would be utopian if it failed to take account from the outset of the unsolved issue of power. Some organizations of recognized general utility like the International Postal Union or the Central Opium Board may indeed achieve a position almost independent of the distribution of power. But these will not by themselves carry us far. The social and economic system of the nineteenth century depended on the unspoken premise of British supremacy. The international agencies of the Second World War were made effective by the joint will and combined power of the principal United Nations. Within what framework of power can a modern

---

[3] Carl Becker, *How New Will the Better World Be?* (1944), pp. 241–3.

international order with its multiplicity of agencies operate? Where will the ultimate decisions be taken that establish or reject its authority? The dream of an international proletarian revolution has faded; and while prophecy may be hazardous, there are few signs at present of any new international group or combination of power splitting national units from within. On the other hand modern developments of power are, though from another standpoint, equally inimical to nationalism in the old sense. These developments, which must now be examined, will go far to determine the shape of the new international order.

POWER IN THE INTERNATIONAL ORDER

Few positive forecasts about the shape of the world after the war can be made with any confidence. But two negative predictions may claim some degree of certainty. We shall not again see a Europe of twenty, and a world of more than sixty, "independent sovereign states", using the term in its hitherto accepted sense; nor shall we see in our time a single world authority as the final repository of power, political and economic, exercising supreme control over the affairs and destinies of mankind. The prospect ahead is a compromise—which, like other compromises, may in the event make either the best or the worst of both worlds—between the past confusion of a vast number of nations, great and small, jostling one another on a footing of formal independence and equality, and the well-knit world authority which may or may not be attainable in the future.

If these predictions are realized, the world will have to accommodate itself to the emergence of a few great multinational units in which power will be mainly concentrated. Culturally, these units may best be called civilizations: there are distinctively British, American, Russian and Chinese civilizations, none of which stops short at national boundaries in the old sense. Economically, the term *Grossraum* invented by German geopoliticians seems the most appropriate. The Soviet Union is pre-eminently a *Grossraum*, the American continents are the potential *Grossraum* of the United States, though the term is less convenient as applied to the British Commonwealth of Nations or the sterling area which are oceanic rather than continental agglomerations. Militarily, the old and useful term "zone of influence" has been discredited and may well have become too weak to express the degree of strategic integration required; but the United States has coined the convenient phrase "hemisphere defence" to cover the zone of influence defined by the Monroe Doctrine. These classifications and divisions are as yet ill-defined. It is difficult to say whether there is a European civilization and a European *Grossraum* or merely a number of separate and conflicting units. Eastern Asia, which Japan once dreamed of organizing as a *Grossraum* under the strange-sounding title of the "co-prosperity sphere", remains fluid. As a civilization China is a closely knit and coherent unit; economically she is weak and depressed; militarily her power is still negligible. India in one sense is a multi-national civilization, in another sense a part of the British unit: her political thought, in particular, is a baffling amalgam of traditional Indian and modem English. In the western hemisphere an older Iberian civilization, still struggling to maintain its ties with Europe, flourishes within the orbit of the modern North American civilization which was itself originally an offshoot from the British unit.

The fact that these actual or prospective agglomerations of power have not yet fully crystallized in such a way as to divide the world between them in clearly defined regional groups provides perhaps the best hope for the future. There would be little cause for congratulation in a division of the world into a small number of large multi-national units exercising effective control over vast territories and practising in competition and conflict with one another a new imperialism which would be simply the old nationalism writ large and would almost certainly pave the way for more titanic and more devastating wars. But international security can ultimately be provided—as well as threatened—only by those who have power, that is to say, for the main part by units having the status, in the old-fashioned but expressive phrase, of "Great Powers". These are a small and perhaps diminishing number; and it is conceivable that, in a world whose social well-being and economic smooth working were adequately promoted by appropriate international organization, the experience of the nineteenth century might repeat itself and no special institution be required for the maintenance of peace and security, which could be settled by ad hoc discussion between the Great Powers from time to time. Two considerations, however, militate against such a solution. In the first place, international security in the modern world is likely to demand the maintenance of some standing international forces made up of different national units; and such a system calls for an institutional framework. Secondly, regulation is required of the relations of great and small nations in a system of pooled security; common membership in a world organization is the right and convenient way of solving a problem which has been made more acute by historical jealousies than by its intrinsic difficulties.

In the eighteenth and nineteenth centuries the convention was well established that issues of war and peace, that is to say, the issues on which security turns, were discussed and decided exclusively by Great Powers. This exclusiveness was not normally resented by the smaller nations; for the counterpart was that, when Great Powers went to war, smaller nations were allowed to remain, subject to the observance of certain rules, in a condition of comfortable neutrality. By 1914 the developments of military technique and economic power had made this immunity of small nations precarious; and recognition of the changed situation inspired in most of them (Switzerland being a striking exception) a desire to make their voice heard in future on issues of peace and war. In the period between the two wars two alternatives seemed open to small countries: to revert to the old policy of unconditional neutrality, and to adhere to the new policy of "collective security", which meant coming to the aid of an attacked country against its attacker.[4] Unfortunately one alternative was as impracticable as the other.

Unconditional neutrality was no longer available: the punctilious anxiety with which Holland and Belgium, Norway and Denmark, Yugoslavia and Greece proclaimed their complete unconcern in the war did not save them from being invaded and occupied. On the other hand collective security was equally unworkable: not a single small country in Europe entered the war until it was itself attacked, not through any lack of wisdom or courage, but because any such step would have been both suicidal and completely purposeless. Small nations could no longer acquire security at the price of neutrality nor could they make any serious contribution to a system of security based on national armed forces taking independent action to be decided on when war actually breaks out.[5]

The two ways out offered to the smaller countries between the two wars—unconditional neutrality and collective security—have thus both been closed[6]; and their survival as independent entities seems incompatible with the maintenance by all nations of wholly independent armed forces which refuse cooperation with those of other powers until a breach of the peace actually occurs. Fortunately the present war, which has thrown this dilemma into high relief and made it a burning issue, also provides the material for a solution. Among the armed forces of the United Nations the process of "mixing up" has been carried far; and on almost every front units of the smaller nations are fighting with those of the three major powers under a common command. In the same way such units may participate with those of Russia, Britain and the United States in the occupation of Germany. Whether this happens or not, the lines of communication of

[4] The difficulties of applying the criterion of "aggression" need not be discussed here, since they did not arise in 1939: even when this additional hurdle had not to be faced, the system proved unworkable.

[5] The argument in this paragraph has been developed at greater length in E. H, Carr, *Conditions of Peace*, pp. 50–60.

[6] The statement may not be universally valid outside Europe; and in Europe itself the conventional "no man's land" of international strife, Switzerland, may remain immune. The prospects of safe neutrality for other neutrals of the Second World War seem less encouraging.

the occupying forces will pass through several countries; and the principle of leased bases initiated during the war can be profitably continued after it.

It is through such haphazard and empirical expedients, rather than through any calculated plan of organization, that we may hope to achieve some rough approximation to the conception of international power. Only in some such way can the smaller nations be enabled to make any effective contribution to a system of international security and to maintain their independence by willingly merging some of its attributes into the common pool.[7]

Such a solution provides the only acceptable answer to the vexed question of national self-determination. As we have seen, the assertion of an alleged right of national self-determination was a development of the nineteenth century. The peace treaties of 1919 were the first large-scale attempt to readjust international frontiers on a principle independent of that of power. The attempt was in some respects faulty. The principle was not always equitably and impartially applied; it was pushed to an extreme through the creation or recognition of impracticably small units; and the assumption was too easily made that language was a test of national allegiance. But recent reactions against national self-determination as a valid principle have been due not to these incidental shortcomings, but to the perception of its apparently radical incompatibility with security. Self-determination raised the issue of military security in the acute form of strategic frontiers. If frontiers were drawn so far as possible to meet the wishes of the populations concerned, they would fail to take account of strategic requirements; if they met strategic requirements, they would ignore the wishes of the inhabitants. The peace-makers of 1919 took on the whole a low view of strategic necessities. The demilitarization of the Rhineland was an awkward compromise, reluctantly adopted to appease

---

[7] An American writer has recently defined the necessary cooperation of large and small nations for common security in terms of the "good neighbour" policy: "The good neighbour relationship is one in which small states and a great one in the same area of strategic security become allies in peace and in war. The great state provides protection which—the technology of modern war being what it is—no small state can provide for itself. The small state reciprocates: it provides strategic facilities needed for the common defence, and it uses its own sovereign powers to protect its great neighbour against infiltration, intrigue and espionage. ... Small nations ... can now assure their rights only by a general acceptance of the duties of the good neighbour policy. We must not, as many do, identify the rights of small nations with their right to have an 'independent' foreign policy, that is to say one which manipulates the balance of power among the great states" (W. Lippmann, *U.S. War Aims*, p. 84).

French insistence. But the wheel has now come full circle. A healthy reaction in favour of the requirements of military security has provoked a correspondingly strong reaction against the principle of self-determination; and notwithstanding its somewhat guarded reaffirmation in the Atlantic Charter, many demands have been heard for its abandonment as the basis of any future territorial settlement. It is true that these specific demands have related mainly to enemy territory. But once the principle were accepted that military considerations were the primary factor in the determination of frontiers, its application could hardly in the long run be restricted to particular cases.

Two powerful arguments seem decisive against such a principle. The first is that there is no such thing as a strategic frontier valid as a permanent bulwark of defence. In 1919 the Rhine was regarded as a strategic frontier of the highest order; in the present war, owing to the use of airborne troops and engineering skill, even the greatest rivers have not proved very formidable obstacles; twenty years hence a river frontier may be strategically worthless. The developments of military technique, and especially of air power, are now so bewilderingly rapid that the impregnable strategic frontier of today, obtained perhaps by flouting the known wishes of millions of people, is only too likely to prove the Maginot Line of to-morrow. The next war, if it is fought at all, will probably be fought in the main with airborne armies and with projectiles having a range of several hundred miles. The whole conception of strategic frontiers may, indeed, be obsolescent; at any rate they can no longer be regarded as a main bulwark of security. The second argument is of a different kind, but not less potent. Self-determination, though it cannot be applied in the meticulous detail aimed at by the peace-makers of 1919, is a principle of good government. Small units can enjoy it only within narrow limits. Larger units cannot enjoy it absolutely and unconditionally; for interdependence is now universal. But the limitations placed on it must be such as appeal to reason and common sense. A peace settlement which transferred tens of millions of people to foreign allegiance—or, worse still, deported them from their homes—in the illusory quest for strategic frontiers might be imposed in the heat of emotion at the end of a bitter and devastating war; but it would not be upheld in cold blood even by the generation that had fought the war, and still less by generations to come. Such a settlement would thus in the long run prove fatal to the security which it sought to achieve.

The issue from this dilemma can be found only through a solution which seeks to divorce international security and the power to maintain it from frontiers and the national sovereignty which they represent. Any international force which could not operate freely across national frontiers would be doomed to inaction. Any system of joint bases in different parts of the world, in which units of different nations may participate, will call for a right of passage across frontiers. If then we can envisage an international order in which frontiers lose their military significance, a ready escape from the dilemma of self-determination is offered; for in the drawing up of national administrative frontiers there will be no case for overriding the wishes of the population, where these are clearly known and defined, on so-called security grounds. Once the military framework of international security is established, the fullest play can be given to these wishes in determining the number, functions and boundaries of the national units exercising authority within it.

This principle provides the only tolerable interpretation which can be placed in practice on the right of national self-determination. National self-determination can hardly hope to survive so long as it is interpreted in a way which nullifies security and limits economic well-being and economic opportunity. But the complexity of human relations fortunately makes it natural and imperative for human beings to combine for various purposes in a variety of groups of varying size and comprehensiveness; and this leaves abundant scope for the development of that community of national thought and feeling, of political and cultural tradition, which is the constructive side of nationalism. The existence of multi-national units of military and economic organization does not stand in the way of the maintenance, or indeed of the further extension, of national administrative and cultural units, thus encouraging a system of overlapping and interlocking loyalties which is in the last resort the sole alternative to sheer totalitarianism.

If, therefore, we seek to define the forms of power in the new international order, the picture we obtain is one of an international general staff, or series of international general staffs for different regions, operating under the general direction of a world security organization with national or joint forces in occupation of strategic bases at key points. It goes without saying that such an organization could function only if the three Great Powers were in agreement to give it their approval and support. It is obvious that it would not in the last resort prevent war between the Great Powers themselves. But it is sheer illusion to suppose that any institution or organization, however perfectly conceived and planned, could achieve this[8]; and the habit of cooperation and common action by the Great Powers would undoubtedly tend to remove a predisposing cause of war between them. It is obvious, too, that such an organization would not be free from the danger of abuses of power. But it is of the essence of power, a defect inherent in its nature and inseparable from it, that it can be abused; and those who, in domestic or in international affairs, would reduce political authority to impotence for fear that power may be abused can offer no alternative to anarchy. The ultimate conditions which will make any international authority tolerable are, first, that it shall maintain order effectively and with reasonable impartiality, and, secondly, that the order it maintains shall serve to promote and protect a widely diffused social well-being. This leads us to an examination of the common principles and common purposes on which any international order must ultimately rest.

---

[8] "War among the founders of the universal society ... cannot be prevented by the rules and procedures of the universal society. ... The world organization cannot police the policemen" (W. Lippmann, *U.S. War Aims*, p. 161).

PRINCIPLES AND PURPOSES

Hitherto the discussion has turned on what may be called the mechanics of international power. But the exercise of authority can never be an end in itself. The settlement of 1919 was strongly influenced by the nineteenth-century doctrine of the laissez-faire state. Those reared in this tradition were likely to take a limited and negative view of the functions of an international organization. Like the state itself, international authority was thought of primarily as something that prevented unnecessary violence and safeguarded the rights of property—a policeman wielding a truncheon in defence of international law and order; its social and economic functions were subsidiary and optional. Today the broader view of freedom involved in its extension from the political to the social and economic sphere calls also for a more positive and constructive view of international authority. The substitution of the "service state" for the "night-watchman state" means that, internationally also, the truncheon must be reinforced by the social agency and subordinated to it. The belief apparently held in some influential quarters that security can be maintained, and war averted, through a perpetual alliance for defence against future aggression from Germany or Japan (who would in the meanwhile, according to most proponents of this view, have been reduced to complete impotence) does not withstand serious examination. Any international order which seeks to conjure the spectre of war and win the allegiance of mankind will have in future to set before it some higher ideal than orderly stagnation. Its primary function will have to be not to maintain the international *status quo* or to defend the rights of nations, but to seek by active policies to improve the conditions of life of ordinary men and women in all countries. No international organization of power, whether it be called a "world security organization" or an "international police force" or by any other name, will prove durable unless it is felt to rest on certain common principles, and to pursue certain common purposes, worthy to command the assent and loyalty of men and women throughout the world.

No thinking man will seek to deny or underestimate the dangers that threaten a world whose fortunes are inevitably dominated by a diminishing number of increasingly powerful units—dangers inherent both in the marked divergences of tradition and outlook and of standards of living and in the potential clashes of interest between them. If, however, we hope—as we rightly do and can hope—to avert these dangers, we must neither seek merely to stabilize an existing situation by artificial measures of security, nor look into the past for our remedies. Taking into account the nature of these great units of power, we must enquire not so much what potential conflicts divide them, but what principles and what purposes they can develop in common. We must seek to build our international order on principles and on purposes which, because they conform to the principles and purposes of the leading powers, will be acceptable to them, and, because they promote the well-being and minister to the aspirations of men and women everywhere, can become the focus of wider loyalties. It is neither necessary nor in the first instance possible that these loyalties should in all cases be world-wide. Organizations for different purposes can be built up on different international groupings whose scope will vary with the functions they perform; and this variety and multiplicity is one of the most important safeguards against the accumulation of exclusive powers and exclusive loyalties under the control of the great multinational units. But common principles and common purposes must be established and resolutely pursued; for these alone can afford the underlying basis of unity which is a condition of international peace.

A modem Spanish writer has defined a nation as "an invitation issued by one group of men to other human groups to carry out some enterprise in common", and has added that contemporary nationalism has failed because it has become "a pretext to escape from the necessity of inventing something new, some great enterprise"[9]—in other words, because it has become an end in itself. An international order which exists merely to defend itself and is unmoved by the ambition to undertake some enterprise in common" will quickly lose all reality and forfeit all respect. Nor is there serious doubt what the "great enterprise" of today should be. It cannot be defined in constitutional terms or expressed in constitutional forms; for it is on the issue of constitutional forms that the nations are most divided. Any project which demands unity on "democratic" or on "communist" lines (to use words both of which have lost something of their pristine clarity of definition) is doomed to failure. Not only is the rivalry between them strong, but there are large areas of the world, including most of Asia and much of Latin America, which seem as far removed from one as from the other. That government should be "popular" and should be broadly based on the consent of the governed is an accepted principle. But there is no general acceptance—perhaps less today than fifty years ago—of the claim of political democracy to provide by itself the only

---

[9] Ortega y Gasset, *The Revolt of the Masses* (English trans., 1932), pp. 183, 197.

and self-sufficient expression of that consent. Nor are political rights and political principles the dominant preoccupation of the contemporary world. The statement often, and justly, made that the future of democracy depends on its ability to solve the problem of full employment illustrates the subordination of political to social and economic ends in the modern world. Internationalism, like nationalism, must become social.

The main unifying purpose in the contemporary world, or in those parts of it where effective flower resides, is the common ideal of social justice latent in such slogans as "the common man", "the worker and the peasant", "the submerged tenth" or "the minimum standard of living Ill-defined though it is, and susceptible of innumerable divergencies of interpretation and application, social justice has assumed in the 20th century the international significance attaching in the previous century to the equally vague but equally powerful concepts of political liberty and political rights. Whereas, however, the political ideals of the 19th century, being attainable by and through the nation, strengthened its political authority and prestige, the national unit seems at best irrelevant to contemporary ideals of social justice and at worst recalcitrant to them. If we seek to analyse what is meant to-day by social justice, we shall find it composed of three main elements—equality of opportunity, "freedom from want" and, as the dynamic factor lending reality to both the other elements, "full employment".

The equality of opportunity which social justice demands is an equality between human beings. It is not merely independent of the demand for equality between nations which wrought havoc and confusion between the two wars, but may be irreconcilable with it; and it can be realized only in a world which rejects the principle of discrimination on grounds of nationality. It would be utopian to suppose that the rejection of the principle would everywhere and immediately lead to a rejection of the practice. Yet the large units of power which confront us in the modem world are not national in the traditional sense; and the kind of internationalism for which they stand at any rate constitutes a step forward from the old nationalism. Whatever differences of outlook and method divide the three Great Powers, they are all united in loyalty to one principle. In the British Commonwealth of Nations one may be an Englishman, Scot or Welshman, a Frenchman or Dutchman, in the United States a German, Pole or Italian, in the Soviet Union a Lithuanian, a Moldavian or a Kazbek without finding any avenue of political and economic opportunity closed on that account, or any barrier placed on devotion to one's own language or national customs. In the Soviet Union the predominant emphasis is laid—except in the sphere of language and culture—not on the national rights of the Kazbek republic, but on the equality enjoyed by the Kazbek throughout the Union with the Uzbek or with the Great Russian.[10] The success of this policy is confirmed by a careful observer in the late 1930s, who reports that "there is such an absence of favour to particular nationalities, and such a constructive effort to make their equality real, that national jealousy and friction are diminished, though not yet eliminated".[11] In the United States full and equal rights are accorded to every citizen irrespective of national origin; but any tendency towards the growth or survival of national consciousness in particular groups is watched with anxiety and any step calculated to encourage it studiously avoided. Moreover, both in the Soviet Union and in the United States a conscious attempt is made, through educational and other channels, to substitute a wider allegiance, conceived in terms of common ideals, for narrower national or racial loyalties—to inculcate the virtues of a Soviet or an American "way of life"; and if the British way of life has been the subject of less positive indoctrination, few will doubt that some such conception, rather than national loyalties in any narrower sense, is the unifying force which has held together a multi-national British Commonwealth of Nations.

It would be rash to deny that these multi-national agglomerations of power are subject to abuses and present dangers of their own—in particular, the danger that they may eventually develop a new imperialism which would be only the old nationalism writ large. Acton once maintained that "the combination of different nations in one state is as necessary a condition of civilized life as the combination of men in society", and that "those states are substantially the most perfect which, like the British and Austrian Empires, include various distinct nationalities without oppressing them".[12] Whether this view be accepted or not, a political unit based not on exclusiveness of nation or language but on shared ideals and aspirations of

---

[10] Act 123 of the 1936 constitution is an emphatic enunciation of this right: "Equality of rights of citizens of the USSR, irrespective of their nationality or race, in all spheres of economic, state, cultural, social and political life, is an indefeasible law. Any direct or indirect restriction of the rights of, or, conversely, any establishment of direct or indirect privileges for, citizens on account of their race or nationality, as well as any advocacy of racial or national exclusiveness or hatred and contempt, is punishable by law."

[11] J. Maynard, *The Russian Peasant and Other Studies*, p. 400.

[12] Acton, *The History of Freedom and Other Essays*, pp. 290, 298.

universal application may be thought to represent a decided advance over a political unit based simply on the cult of a nation, or even over a political unit like pre-1939 Yugoslavia or Poland, where it made all the difference in the world whether one was a Serb, Croat or Slovene, a Pole, Ukrainian or Lithuanian.[13] It would seem therefore that, whatever other forms of human intolerance may become prominent, the expansion of the power and influence of great multi-national units must encourage the spread of national toleration. The oft-quoted parallel of religion and nationalism would suggest that, just as the movement for religious toleration followed the devastating religious wars of the sixteenth and seventeenth centuries, so the movement for national toleration will spring—since there is no reason to suppose that mankind has lost the will to survive—from the destructive twentieth-century wars of nationalism. The shift in emphasis from the rights and well-being of the national group to the rights and well-being of the individual man and woman which we already see at work in the multi-national state, if it could now be transferred to the sphere of international organization, would mark the beginning of the end of the destructive phase of nationalism.

The second element in social justice—"freedom from want"—is more familiar, more concrete and requires less discussion. It could indeed be argued that freedom from want is often as easily attainable by suitable policies within the nation as by international cooperation. In some cases "this is, broadly speaking, true. But just as the social conscience calls today for mitigation of extremes of wealth. and poverty among classes within the nation, so it has begun to recognize the close juxtaposition of nations with widely divergent standards of living as a menace to peace and to seek mitigation of such conditions as one of the initial constructive tasks of an international order. On the other hand, it would be utopian to seek the attainment of this goal through universal or uniform action and organization. The issue presents a striking illustration of the need for adapting social policies to social conditions. The ideal of, freedom from want is universal. But the problems of its application to advanced regions with a relatively inelastic birth-rate will be different not merely in degree, but in kind, from those of its application to regions where population constantly presses on a marginal level of subsistence. No single issue reveals more

---

[13] It is fair, however, to recall examples of perfect equality between nations in smaller multi-national states, notably Switzerland, and of discrimination against coloured people in some parts of the British Commonwealth and in the United States.

starkly the underlying lack of homogeneity which blocks the way to realization of the ideal of world unity and imposes division and diversity of policy in the pursuit even of aims recognized as common to mankind.

The third element—full employment—holds a somewhat paradoxical place in the contemporary programme of social justice. In one sense it is not an end in itself, since employment is always employment for some purpose, and nothing is more barren than the notion that the cure for unemployment is to provide otherwise unwanted "public works". In another sense, however, full employment is the master key to social justice in the modern industrial state, the dynamic force which alone can cure the major social evils of our time; and for this reason the central place occupied by it in modern thought is fully justified. The dependence of freedom from want on full employment is immediate and obvious; for though the breakdown of the economic system has been more conspicuous on the side of distribution than on that of production, it remains true that the wide extension of higher standards of living can be made possible only by increased production, and that this in turn demands the full employment of all resources, human and material. But it is less commonly recognized that full employment is also a primary condition of that equality of opportunity between man and man which we have recognized as the first element of social justice. Unemployment or fear of unemployment has been the most fertile cause of exclusion and discrimination in the modern world. It has sharpened and barbed every restrictive instrument of economic and financial policy; it has dammed and severely restricted the flow of migration from country to country; it has intensified discrimination against minorities, often raising it to the pitch of organized persecution; it has closed almost every door to refugees. Unemployment has been the specific social scourge of the contemporary western world and takes a high place among the ultimate causes of the Second World War. It will serve no purpose to inveigh against these evils if the condition which produced them is allowed to recur. Full employment is the only solvent powerful enough to break down the static and restrictive policies which dominated western civilization before 1939 and enable the present generation to build a social and international order on new and firmer foundations of equality of opportunity and freedom from want.

There would be no insuperable difficulty in drawing up ambitious international plans to assure full employment throughout the world, though even such plans could not be uniform, since backward and undeveloped countries would inevitably appear in them as objects rather than as originators of policy. But as a matter of practical politics, the prospects of making effective provision for full employment by agreements or machinery of world-wide scope are slender. Diversities in technical and economic development, with the conflicts of interest which these create, are too great to permit of a completely homogeneous system; and it is a symptom of these diversities that agreement about ends is not matched by agreement about means. Here again we shall probably have to be content with systems of joint planning and organization between countries or groups of countries agreeing to pursue full employment policies in common, or to share in the economic development of backward areas; and such regional policies may correspond in part, though not necessarily or exclusively, with the multi-national groupings of power. The stability of the framework of international order will thus come to depend partly on the balance of forces between the Great Powers, and partly on the success of common policies directed towards the realization of equality of opportunity, of freedom from want and of full employment. It is an illusion to suppose that security for the individual or for the nation can be attained through the limited resources of the small or medium-sized nation-states or through the untrammelled and independent action of national governments. It is equally an illusion to suppose that the demands of social justice can be attained through a return to the "free" international market economy of the nineteenth century. To achieve these results through an executive world authority planning, directing and controlling from a single centre remains a dream of visionaries. The best hope of achieving them in the next period lies in a balanced structure of international or multi-national groupings both for the maintenance of security and for the planned development of the economies of geographical areas and groups of nations. This seems the surest prospect of international advance open, at one of the crises of history, to a world bewildered by the turmoil of nationalism and war.

Postscript

In this pattern of the modern world, dominated by new concentrations of power in great groups of nations, but crossed with strands of common social and economic policy and woven loosely together in a system of pooled security, the position of Great Britain is unique, and not free from anxiety. By herself, Great Britain is no match for the other great multinational units and, with a population about the decline steeply, might be well on the way to become a secondary power. Were this to happen, British policy would be faced by a fearful dilemma; it would have the choice of subordinating itself to the policy either of the Soviet Union or of the United States, or of attempting, as other secondary powers have done in the past, to play off the more powerful units against one another—with inevitably disastrous results. But if this is not to happen, Britain must fulfil two conditions.

In the first place, a considered policy of economic and social organization is required to bring about that marked increase of efficiency in the production and distribution of wealth which will alone enable Britain to retain a leading place in the affairs of the world and convince other nations of her ability to retain it, and it would be reckless to underestimate the opposition to this far-reaching readjustment which will come from traditional inertia as well as from vested interests. Secondly, British conceptions of international policy must be radically changed. In this field, Britain has

E.H. Carr, *Nationalism and After*,
https://doi.org/10.1057/978-1-349-96038-5

a great potential source of strength, not only in the reinforcement which the British Commonwealth of Nations brings to her position but also in the lesson that can be drawn from inter-Commonwealth relations. These do not rest on treaties or on formal obligations; even the follies of the treaty-ridden period between the two wars left relations between members of the Commonwealth unaffected. The crucial lesson of the Commonwealth can now be given a wider application. In relations with members of the Commonwealth, with nations which had already before 1939 been drawn into the fraternity of the sterling area, and with other friendly nations which may in future be drawn into a close community of interest with them, Britain should proceed not by way of generalized international engagements or long-term mutual guarantees, but by way of agreements issuing in direct and specific common action, of military conventions involving joint planning by a common General Staff and of trade agreements which approximate more closely to commercial transactions than to international treaties in the time-honoured form. These are the international policies which, combined with industrial and social reconstruction at home, will entitle Britain not only to retain a leading position among the nations of the world but to make a first and constructive contribution to the creation of a lasting international order.

Among the nations with whom Britain might perhaps establish closer relations of this kind are those of Western Europe. The plight of Western Europe is graver than that of Great Britain, and is in some respects tragic. In the first place, Western Europe is the home of the "national" epoch from which the world is now emerging. It is organized on a basis whose military and economic foundations have been irrevocably sapped—the basis of independent nations, each tenaciously clinging to its own traditional civilization, and either the sudden downfall or the slow decay of a powerful and traditional form of organization which has been overtaken by events and rendered obsolete is inevitably marked with tragedy. Secondly, Western Europe, even if she can renew her vitality and escape from the thrall of traditions once glorious, but now stifling to fresh growth, still lacks the leadership and central focus of power which would be necessary to place her among the great multi-national civilizations of the "hemisphere" or *Grossraum* epoch. Both Italy and France have in the past laid some of the foundations of a common European civilization, but both abused their power and fell behind in the race. In the nineteenth-century Germany developed some of the qualifications for the leadership of a modem industrial Europe, but Germany has irretrievably abused her power. As the Second World War comes to its end the unprecedented position has arisen that the two European powers most able to influence the destinies of Europe—Russia and Britain—are situated at its eastern and western extremities and are not exclusively or primarily European powers at all.

The outlook remains, therefore, dark and uncertain. It is conceivable that a shattered Europe, rising above the national hatreds and conflicts of the past, may throw up from within a new and unifying leadership which would enable her to develop and hold a position independent of both Britain and Russia. But no such prospect is yet visible above the horizon; and failing this, it seems likely that the European nations will inevitably be drawn into closer relations with both Russia and Britain. There are already signs of such an association between Russia and the nations of Eastern Europe. A natural corollary would be the establishment of more intimate links, couched in terms appropriate to the western tradition, between Britain and the nations of Western Europe. Such links, military and economic rather than political in the narrower sense, would rest on a solid basis of common interest. The same problems of security are common to the whole region. Most of them are faced with the same problems of economic readjustment arising from balance of payments in dislocation, a high degree of independence on foreign trade, and a developed industry working on imported raw materials. The same challenge of social justice will be encountered and accepted by them all; and they may be united by the same desire to find an answer based on principles which diverge both from the Soviet ideology of state monopoly and from the American ideology of unrestricted competition. Several of them have vast dependent colonial territories, the greater part of the African continent being divided between them. Common economic planning, as well as joint military organization, will alone enable Western Europe, Britain included, to confront the future with united strength and confidence. The pride and prejudice of ancient traditions, as well as the innate conservatism of those who refuse to believe that the past cannot return, stand in the way of such a course. But many old traditions will have to be discarded, and new ones created, before Europe and the world can recover their balance in the aftermath of the age of nationalism.